SECRETS OF
MACARONS

First published by Marabout in 2010

Reprinted in 2020

This edition published in 2010 by Murdoch Books Pty Limited

Murdoch Books Australia
Pier 8/9
23 Hickson Road
Millers Point NSW 2000
Phone: +61 (0) 2 8220 2000
Fax: +61 (0) 2 8220 2558
www.murdochbooks.com.au

Murdoch Books UK Limited
Erico House, 6th Floor
93–99 Upper Richmond Road
Putney, London SW15 2TG
Phone: +44 (0) 20 8785 5995
Fax: +44 (0) 20 8785 5985
www.murdochbooks.co.uk

Translator: Melissa McMahon
Editor: Emma Driver
Project editor: Laura Wilson
Cover design: Katy Wall
Production: Joan Beal

Text and design © Marabout 2010
Front cover photograph © Riou/photocuisine/Corbis

National Library of Australia Cataloguing-in-Publication Data
Title: Secrets of macarons.
Author   José Maréchal
ISBN: 978-1-74266-128-5 (hbk.)
Notes: Includes index.
Subjects: Cookies.
Dewey Number: 641.8654

MIX
Paper from
responsible sources
FSC
www.fsc.org   FSC® C008047

A catalogue record for this book is available from the British Library.

Printed in China by C&C Offset Printing Co., Ltd.

IMPORTANT: Those who might be at risk from the effects of salmonella poisoning (the elderly, pregnant women, young children and those suffering from immune deficiency diseases) should consult their doctor with any concerns about eating raw eggs.

OVEN GUIDE: You may find cooking times vary depending on the oven you are using. For fan-forced ovens, as a general rule, set the oven temperature to 20°C (35°F) lower than indicated in the recipe.

SECRETS OF MACARONS

JOSÉ MARÉCHAL
Photography by FRÉDÉRIC LUCANO

MURDOCH BOOKS

PREFACE

INTRODUCED TO FRANCE *from Italy in the 16th century by Catherine de' Medici, the macaron was originally a form of pasta. The evolution of the macaron has transformed it into a pâtisserie treat.*

The recipe for the macaron — now a biscuit made from almonds, sugar and egg whites — spread quickly, and by the 17th century it was found in many French towns, including Nancy, Amiens, Saint-Émilion and Montmorillon.

Now a worldwide symbol of dainty indulgence, the macaron seduces tastebuds and practically invites itself onto our plates.

This small round biscuit, crisp and tender at the same time, has transcended generations and is more in-vogue than ever. Gourmands can let go of their guilt because the macaron represents just a little "mouthful" to lift the spirits. Even allergy-sufferers can fall in love with this gluten-free treat.

The infatuation for this must-have small sweet is thus far from finished, and we can always pay homage by creating new flavours.

In a thorough approach to the subject, in this book I try to offer some tips and tricks, an analysis of what can go wrong, and a considered selection of the necessary equipment and ingredients. Every step is explained simply, to maximise your chances of success. Rest assured that macarons are no harder to achieve at home than a choux or flaky pastry.

Take pleasure in making these little biscuits, let yourself be guided by your fancy, and treat yourself to this little luxury that you can (almost) consume without moderation!

*

TABLE OF CONTENTS

CHAPTER 1

INGREDIENTS & TECHNIQUES

*The macaron is a delicate almond-flavoured morsel, like a meringue
with a melting heart of butter, chocolate or fruit.*

THE ALMOND

*The almond is an oleaginous (oily) seed with a pale and crunchy flesh
that can be sweet or bitter (in the case of wild almonds)*

COMPOSITION

THE FRUIT OF the almond tree, the almond is a nut enclosed in a green pod, as downy to the touch as a peach.

When it is harvested in early summer, the fruit is not ripe: it is hard and not juicy.

Its thick shell encloses a kernel called an almond, a precious seed with a high oil content, which is edible in various forms.

For macarons, ground almonds are used. Almond meal is made by grinding blanched almonds, and is widely available in stores.

The nutritional information for 100 g (3½ oz) almonds:

Water .... 2.6 g (¹/16 oz)	Carbohydrates ....5.6 g (¹/8 oz)	Magnesium....... 2.3 g (¹/16 oz)
Protein.............. 23.6 g (1 oz)	Fats................. 52.9 g (1³/4 oz)	**Energy ...... 2490 kJ (593 cal)**

THE ORIGINS OF THE ALMOND

THE ALMOND TREE is thought to have originated in the warm and dry regions of the Near and Middle East. It was introduced to Spain by the Arabs, and from there spread throughout the Mediterranean Basin. It had to wait until the middle of the 18th century for Spanish Franciscan monks to take it to North America, or, more precisely, to California.

Today, California is the world's largest almond producer, closely followed by Spain.

ALMONDS: A NATURAL DIETARY SUPPLEMENT

HIGH IN FIBRE, protein, minerals and vitamins E and B12, almonds are a substitute for many dietary supplements — at a much more economical price.

Almonds protect our bodies from the accumulation of excess acid due to an unbalanced diet high in sugar, fat and animal proteins. They contribute to the prevention of cardiovascular disease, osteoporosis and obesity. They help to lower levels of "bad" cholesterol in the body, restore energy to sufferers of malnutrition and are a safe substitute for people with food allergies (in particular to gluten, lactose, etc.).

For these reasons, almonds have a natural role to play in our daily diet, especially in vegetarian cuisine.

Did you know? 30 g (1 oz) almonds provides as much protein as a tub of yoghurt or a glass of milk.

THE ALMOND: A USER'S GUIDE

HOW ARE SWEET ALMONDS USED?

THE FIRST FRESH, sweet almonds of the season, "green almonds", are enjoyed as a dessert.

The dried kernel (whole, roasted, flaked, crushed, or in the form of a paste, cream or milk) is eaten as is, or used as an ingredient in a wide range of cakes, biscuits, sweets and confectionery (sugared almonds, nougat, marzipan, frangipane and orgeat syrup (see glossary)).

But almonds aren't limited to sweet dishes: they are often served with meat and fish, and flavour savoury dishes such as stuffings, pestos and flavoured butters.

ARE BITTER ALMONDS EDIBLE?

DRIED BITTER ALMONDS are poisonous in large quantities because they contain hydrogen cyanide (Prussic acid). Small quantities are, however, used in pastry making and confectionery, for example in the famous *coucougnette* sweets from the French town of Pau.

AND FOR MACARONS?

GROUND ALMONDS, WHICH are widely available, are processed with more or less equal quantities of icing sugar depending on the type of recipe (Italian or French meringue). The resulting mixture is called the *tant pour tant* (literally: "so much for so much").

CAN I USE WHOLE ALMONDS AND GRIND THEM MYSELF?

YES. THE FLAVOUR will be stronger but it will take a little more time.

Drop whole almonds into boiling water and leave them for 2 minutes, then drain. To remove their skin, squeeze the almonds between your thumb and index finger.

Roughly chop the almonds with a knife or in the food processor, then dry them out in the oven for 10 minutes at 120°C (235°F/ Gas ½). Keep an eye on them because they mustn't colour.

Once the almonds have cooled, process them until you have a fine powder. Make sure you don't overload the processor: it is better to grind the almonds in several batches because they contain a lot of oil and there's a risk that they'll turn into a paste. Return the ground almonds to the oven (120°C/235°F/Gas ½ with fan-forced setting turned off) for 10 minutes.

Once cooled, process and sift with the icing sugar.

WHY DO YOU NEED TO PROCESS AND/OR SIFT THE *TANT POUR TANT*?

THE GROUND ALMONDS are processed with the icing sugar to create a fine powder. This stage shouldn't be skipped because it gives you a smooth batter, without any lumps.

The macaron shells will be smooth and shiny as a result. Once the *tant pour tant* is processed, you just need to sift it using a fine strainer or drum sieve.

*Macaron shell using unprocessed
tant pour tant.*

*Macaron shell using processed
tant pour tant.*

CAN THE *TANT POUR TANT* BE MADE IN ADVANCE?

YES. ONCE MADE, store in an airtight container in a dry place away from moisture until ready to use. This small time-saving measure will make a difference on macaron-making day. Make sure, however, that you don't keep it for too long because even when combined with the sugar, the flavour of the almonds can spoil.

HOW DO YOU MAKE
THE ALMOND PASTE?

THE MACARON BATTER is made by incorporating Italian meringue into an almond paste.

To make the almond paste, you need to incorporate egg white into the *tant pour tant* using a silicon spatula. It needs to be mixed together well to make a smooth, pliable and fairly thick paste.

It's this paste that colourings are added to in order to make coloured macarons.

THE EGG

The egg is one of the most nutritious foods, with multiple uses in many kinds of cooking

COMPOSITION

THE EGG IS made up of a shell, a spherical yolk and a clear, viscous liquid. Chalazae, the threads of albumin protein located on either side of the yolk, hold it in place in the middle of the white.

The shell represents about 10% of the weight of the egg. It is porous, fragile and permeable to moisture, odours and air. Lined with a membrane made from 2 or 3 protein fibres, it remains a protective barrier against bacteria.

The yolk, which represents 30% of the egg, contains 50% water, about 17% protein and 33% fat, including lecithin.

The white part makes up about two-thirds of the egg. It is made up of 87% water, 12% albumin (protein), and 1% fats and vitamins. It is transparent and water-soluble.

THE ROLES PLAYED BY EGG WHITE AND EGG YOLK

EGG WHITE IS mostly made up of water, but also contains proteins, the main one being ovalbumin. Its interest lies in its coagulative properties (between 60 and 65°C/140 and 150°F), which thicken and solidify mixtures, and its surfactant properties, which stabilise the foam of beaten egg whites.

The yolk contains proteins and fats, including lecithin, which has an emulsifying effect that helps with the texture, softness and keeping properties of culinary preparations. By itself, it coagulates between 65 and 70°C (150 and 160°F); diluted in a liquid, between 80 and 85°C (175 and 185°F).

THE EGG: A USER'S GUIDE

EGG SIZES

IN BAKING AND especially for macarons, it's best, for accuracy, to weigh out the amount of egg white or yolk required. In this book, I have provided the weight for egg whites in each recipe. As a guide, a "medium" whole egg weighs 50 g (1³/4 oz); 1 yolk = approximately 20 g (³/4 oz); 1 white = approximately 30 g (1 oz).

HOW SHOULD EGG WHITES AND YOLKS BE STORED?

WHOLE EGGS in their shell keep in the refrigerator for up to 5 weeks from the date packed.

Whites (separated from the yolks) can be kept in an airtight container in the refrigerator for 5 to 6 days, and for 6 to 10 months in the freezer.

Egg yolks are more perishable. They should be used straight away or kept in the refrigerator for a maximum of 24 hours.

French meringue, ready to use.

FRENCH MERINGUE

HOW DO YOU BEAT EGG WHITES TO SOFT PEAKS?

It is very important to use equipment that's clean and absolutely dry.

The tiniest bit of egg yolk can interfere with the development of the foam. Use egg whites at room temperature, separated the day before (refrigerated overnight, and brought back to room temperature). Beat them in a cold mixing bowl. It is better to begin by beating gently and then gradually increase the speed. The effect of the fast, repetitive action is to incorporate air into the egg whites, in the form of ever-smaller bubbles.

This action also "denatures" the proteins by dispersing and imprisoning them between tiny bubbles of air and water. This creates a white and airy foam: fluffy beaten egg whites.

WHAT IS THE EFFECT OF SUGAR ON THE EGG WHITES?

The addition of sugar gives structure to the beaten egg whites.

It surrounds the egg-white proteins and prevents them from binding together too much. This slows down the development of the foam but also allows the whites to be beaten for longer. The air bubbles become finer and more stable.

The sugar stabilises the water in the foam, which becomes more pliable and stable.

Shell made from French meringue (uncooked sugar).

MACARONS USING FRENCH MERINGUE?

French meringue, using uncooked sugar, is simpler to make than Italian meringue, because the sugar doesn't need to be cooked to a precise temperature.

Making macaron shells using a French meringue, however, requires more care. In effect, since French meringue is more fragile, the process of working the macaron batter (the *macaronage*) needs to be much more precise in order to obtain smooth shells without cracks.

An Italian meringue (see page 22), on the other hand, is more complex to make, but ensures a silkier batter. It also allows you to cook the macaron shells at a lower temperature, which preserves the colour and shine of the macarons.

SUGAR

Sugar is extracted from sugar beets or sugar cane

COMPOSITION

SUGAR OR SACCHAROSE is formed from two molecules: one of fructose and one of glucose.

In its solid or crystallised state, sugar is a colourless and odourless substance which has, of course, a sweet taste.

Both brown and white sugar can be derived from sugar cane or sugar beets. There is no relationship between the colour of the sugar and the plant it is extracted from.

Caster sugar is obtained from grinding and sifting crystallised white sugar. It contains 99.7% purified and crystallised saccharose.

Icing sugar is a white powder made by grinding crystallised white sugar very finely, sometimes with added starch so it doesn't clump together. The fineness of its grains makes it the sugar that dissolves quickest.

Soft brown sugar is a raw sugar, or a refined one with added colour. Unlike white sugar, soft brown sugar contains traces of vitamins and minerals, but these elements are present in such tiny quantities as to be insignificant for the human body.

Jam sugar, also called gelling sugar, is a crystallised sugar to which natural fruit pectin and citric acid have been added. In cooking, this helps mixtures to set more easily.

One tonne of beetroot yields an average of 140 kg (310 lb) sugar.

One tonne of sugar cane yields an average of 115 kg (255 lb) sugar.

Nutritional information for 100 g (3¹/₂ oz) caster sugar:

Carbohydrate... 100 g (3¹/₂ oz)	Protein................... 0 g (0 oz)	**Energy ...... 1675 kJ (400 cal)**
Mineral salts......... 30–50 mg	Fats....................... 0 g (0 oz)	

THE ROLES PLAYED BY SUGAR

SUGAR DOESN'T JUST add flavour. It also partly conditions the look and texture of the finished product.

Sugar is hygroscopic, meaning that it binds and holds water molecules. As such it promotes the development of foams, stabilises beaten egg whites by preventing the proteins from over-binding and slows down loss of moisture from preparations during cooking.

At high temperatures, sugar caramelises and its aromatic notes develop.

Combined with protein (the Maillard reaction), sugar gives a brown colour, adds "body" and contributes to the consistency of certain baked goods.

Since it helps retain the carbon dioxide produced by raising agents, sugar allows an airier crumb to be achieved in products like sandwich bread.

SUGAR: A USER'S GUIDE

CAN HONEY BE USED IN PLACE OF CASTER SUGAR?

HONEY IS 100% natural. It is made up of fructose and glucose, two simple sugars (monosaccharides) that help digestion.

In uncooked dishes, honey can replace sugar, but since it is a more powerful sweetener, the amount used should be reduced a little.

Cooking with honey is a more delicate matter, because it tends to crystallise when heated and colour more quickly. It loses its nutritional qualities but keeps all of its advantages in terms of taste, especially in an Italian meringue (used for macarons, nougats, glacés and honey meringues).

WHAT IS THE EFFECT OF SUGAR ON BEATEN EGG WHITES?

WHEN YOU BEAT egg whites, you incorporate microscopic air bubbles and the proteins open out to form a film around each of them. A light foam forms, but it remains fragile and unstable. Prolonged beating risks damaging these air bubbles. Adding sugar strengthens the structure of the egg whites to form a meringue. It surrounds the egg-white proteins and prevents them binding with each other too much, allowing them to be beaten for longer.

In addition, sugar attracts and binds the moisture in the foam, stopping it from running to the bottom of the bowl. The meringue is therefore more stable and stays moist and pliable for longer.

WHAT PRECAUTIONS SHOULD BE TAKEN WHEN MAKING A SUGAR SYRUP?

USE A CLEAN saucepan with a thick and very flat base, and ensure there is no trace of fat on it.

Gently heat the sugar–water mixture with a few drops of white vinegar or lemon juice. Gently shake the saucepan to dissolve the sugar, then increase the temperature.

Clean the side of the saucepan with a damp pastry brush to avoid crystallisation.

When the syrup reaches the desired stage of cooking, remove from the heat and dip the base of the saucepan in cold water for a few seconds to stop the sugar cooking any further.

THE DIFFERENT STAGES OF COOKING SUGAR

COMBINED WITH WATER and vinegar, and under the effect of heat, sugar changes. Between 100°C (210°F) (the temperature at which sugar dissolves completely and the syrup becomes perfectly transparent) and 200°C (390°F) (the temperature at which it carbonises) sugar takes on a variety of forms, from a syrup to a caramel.

If you don't have a thermometer, take a little bit of syrup on a small spoon and drop it quickly into cold, clean water, then feel the sugar between your thumb and forefinger to test its consistency. In this way, you will be able to judge the cooking stage the syrup has reached, and make Italian meringues, macarons and other dishes.

SUGAR-COOKING TABLE

STAGE	TEMPERATURE	APPEARANCE AND BEHAVIOUR	USES
Syrup	105°C (220°F)	The syrup starts to boil and becomes transparent; it coats a skimmer dipped in the syrup	For soaking babas, biscuits, fruits in syrup, jams, jellies and marmalades
Thread or soft ball	110–115°C (230–240°F)	A drop of syrup between thumb and index finger forms a small thread when fingers open	Butter creams, fruit jellies and fruit pastes
Firm ball	116–125°C (240–255°F)	A little syrup dropped from a spoon into a bowl of water forms a soft and pliable ball	Butter creams, parfaits, soufflés, marrons glacés, candied fruit, Italian meringues and macarons
Hard ball	126–135°C (255–275°F)	The ball is very firm	Soft fondants and caramels
Soft crack	136–140°C (275–285°F)	The ball breaks and stays sticky	Hard fondant, soft marzipans and soft caramels
Hard crack	145–155°C (295–310°F)	The ball is hard and brittle but not sticky	Marzipans, nougats, sweets and caramels
Caramel	160-177°C (230-350°F)	The sugar turns golden and becomes browner	Nougats, pulled and blown sugar decorations, spun sugar, glazed fruit

A sugar syrup at 115°C (240°F).

Crystallised sugar.

ITALIAN MERINGUE

WHAT IS ITALIAN MERINGUE?

ITALIAN MERINGUE IS beaten egg whites to which a sugar syrup at the "soft ball" 110–115°C (230–240°F) stage is added.

Syrup that isn't hot enough will form an unstable foam; too hot and it will crystallise and won't combine with the egg whites.

WHY USE ITALIAN MERINGUE TO MAKE THE MACARON SHELLS, RATHER THAN FRENCH MERINGUE?

SINCE THE SUGAR is incorporated in the form of a syrup, it disperses into the beaten egg whites well, puffing them up while evaporating some moisture. The sugar envelops the air bubbles and holds the foam together, making the meringue smoother and shinier.

Since Italian meringue has a denser consistency, it is easier to incorporate into the almond paste. It has a less brittle structure and the *macaronage* (working the batter) is more manageable. The cooked macaron keeps a stronger meringue-like appearance and stays soft.

With French meringue, since the sugar is incorporated "cold", the structure of the whites is wetter and more aerated, and it is therefore a more delicate job to incorporate a large quantity of the *tant pour tant* without collapsing the foam. There's the danger of the batter becoming too runny or, at the other end of the spectrum, lumpy.

French meringue also needs more time to form a crust and more attention needs to be paid to the cooking. Once cooked, the macaron is more "brittle", with less-defined colour and shape. The taste, however, is not affected.

Pour in the syrup when the whites become frothy.

Macaron shell made from Italian meringue (with cooked sugar).

The meringue should be shiny and form a peak on the whisk.

COLOURING

POWDER, PASTE OR LIQUID?

Powdered colours: these are not very practical because they are very volatile and difficult to measure out. They are used to make really bright colours. Gold and silver leaf and edible shimmer powders can also be used after cooking (see page 48).

Paste colours: these are ideal and their colouring power is amazing. They mix together well and allow you to create subtle shades. Be careful not to overdo the quantity, which could alter the consistency of the batter.

Liquid colours: these are more delicate to use and only produce soft and pastel colours. It is recommended you only use a few drops to colour the meringue (French meringue macarons) or almond paste (Italian meringue macarons).

Macaron flavour	Colours used
Lemon, orange	Lemon yellow, egg yellow, orange
Berry	Red, raspberry, pink, wine
Lime, pistachio, mint	Green (adjust with lemon yellow depending on the type of green)
Coffee, caramel, praline, walnut	Coffee extract, caramel, cream, brown + yellow
Milk or dark chocolate	Cocoa added to the paste, dark brown, light brown (+ red)
Blackcurrant, blueberry, fig	Wine, violet, red + 1 dash blue
Apricot, blood orange, exotic	Egg yellow, orange, paprika or red + yellow
Vanilla, plain, white chocolate	White (titanium dioxide in powder or paste form)

Colouring plus almond paste.

The effect in the mixed batter.

A panorama of colours.

Once well combined, the batter is a lighter shade than the initial colouring.

MACARONAGE (WORKING THE BATTER)

HOW DO YOU INCORPORATE THE MERINGUE INTO THE ALMOND PASTE?

Using a flexible spatula, first incorporate a small quantity of meringue into the almond paste to loosen it a little. Then add the rest of the meringue using a regular action, moving from the bottom towards the top and from the edges towards the centre of the bowl.

This stage is fundamental: it's what's called the *macaronage*. It is a matter of working the batter in order to lightly "break" the meringue (unlike soufflé, mousse or cake recipes, where egg whites must be folded in very gently to keep their lightness). The resulting mixture should be smooth, uniform and gently flowing (see photo opposite).

Be careful however not to overdo it, or else the batter will be too runny (photo at bottom right). The macarons will then be too flat and not have their ruffled "feet".

The batter is ready to be piped.

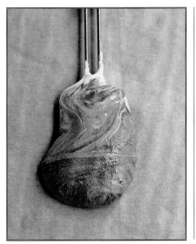

The batter is not uniform enough.

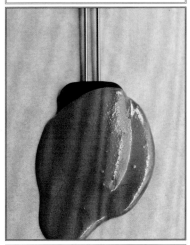

The batter is too runny.

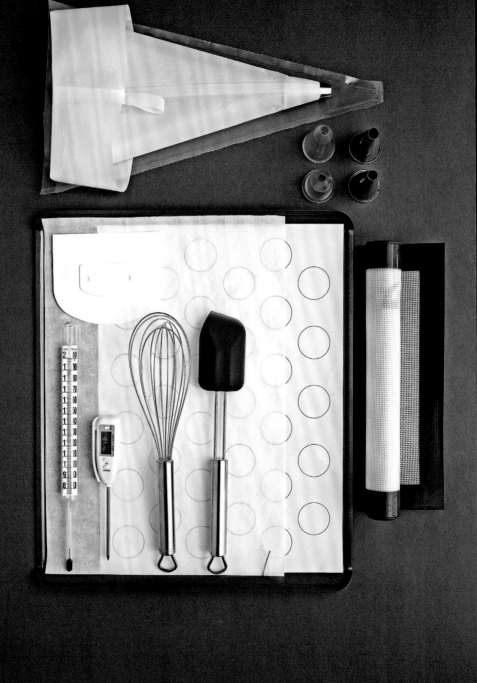

THE EQUIPMENT

A small number of basic tools are needed for successful baking

KITCHEN OR ELECTRONIC SCALES

PRECISION IS NECESSARY when making macarons — so, no "near enough" when measuring. A few grams more or less can make a considerable difference to the consistency of the meringue and the look of your macarons.

FOOD PROCESSOR AND SIEVE

THESE ARE USED for processing the icing sugar–almond mixture and eliminating lumps that could form unattractive blisters on the surface of the macaron shell.

ELECTRIC MIXER OR BEATER

A STAND MIXER offers the advantage of leaving your hands free while you're waiting for the egg whites to form peaks. With a hand-held electric beater, beat the whites using a regular circular movement: they will come together better and more quickly.

THERMOMETER

To MAKE COOKED-SUGAR macarons, use a sugar thermometer graduated from 80 to 200°C (175 to 390°F), or an electric probe thermometer (more precise but expensive).

RUBBER OR SILICON SPATULA

THIS IS THE essential tool for incorporating the meringue into the almond paste with- out damaging the egg whites too much. It allows more precision in your action.

PIPING BAG AND NOZZLES

PIPING BAGS COME in nylon, laminated fabric or, better still, disposable plastic. You can find them in speciality stores or online. The nozzles, which are made from moulded plastic or stainless steel, are the essential components of the bag. For macarons, use a plain nozzle 8 mm ($^3/_8$ in) or 10 mm ($^1/_2$ in) wide.

OVEN AND BAKING TRAYS

A FAN-FORCED OVEN is preferable. It will probably be necessary to adjust the temperature by a few degrees or vary the cooking time by a few minutes. Use baking trays that are fairly thick and quite flat. Line them with baking paper or a silicone mat. Turn them around halfway through the cooking time for even baking.

THE PIPING BAG

USING THE PIPING BAG PROPERLY

1. CUT OFF THE tip of the bag (3 cm/1¼ in), then insert the nozzle. Be careful not to cut off too much or the nozzle will slip through and the bag will be unuseable.

2. Fold some of the bag inside the nozzle, pushing the plastic down, to make a "stopper" so that the batter doesn't ooze out the nozzle when you fill the bag.

3. Before filling the bag, stabilise the container holding the batter — with a tea towel, for example.

4. Fold down half the bag over your hand. This allows you to hold the bag firmly and also to fill it cleanly.

5. Scoop up some batter with a silicon spatula or plastic scraper. Place it inside the bag then wipe off the spatula or scraper. Only fill the bag with batter to halfway.

6. Once the bag is filled, roll the end of the bag back up and give it a quarter-turn, pushing the batter towards the nozzle with the palm of the hand.

7. To pipe out: hold the bag in one hand and the nozzle in the other hand, which will help guide your movements. Gently pull on the nozzle to remove the "stopper", then pipe the macarons onto the tray by gently pressing with the palm of your hand. Compress the batter as you go along by giving the bag another quarter-turn each time.

TIP: if you need both hands to fill or refill the bag, use a high-walled container such as a vase, or a plastic bottle with the end cut off, as a support.

The bag is ready to be filled.

To refill the bag easily,
sit it inside a cut-off plastic bottle.

The bag has been filled and, thanks to the "stopper", the batter doesn't ooze out.

PIPING

HOW DO YOU MAKE REGULAR MACARON SHELLS?

To HELP YOU pipe macarons that are nice and regular and the same size, all you need to do is take a pen or pencil and a glass or cookie-cutter, and draw staggered rows of circles, 3.5 cm (1¹/₂ in) wide, on baking paper. These can be used as a template for the macarons.

Cover this template with another sheet of baking paper (join them together with a paperclip if necessary).

PIPING IN PRACTICE

HOLD THE BAG with one hand and the nozzle with the other, which will help guide your movements.

Gently pull on the nozzle to remove the "stopper" that was made using the bag, then pipe small flat rounds inside each drawn circle, applying light pressure with the palm of your hand.

Compress the batter by tightening the bag with a quarter-turn each time.

HOW DO YOU ATTACH THE PAPER TO THE TRAY?

PUT SMALL dots of batter on the tray to prevent the paper lifting up during cooking. Place the paper onto the tray.

Once the macarons have been piped onto the paper, lightly tap the bottom of the tray to smooth out the surface of the macarons.

Pipe rounds of batter onto the baking paper, following the template.

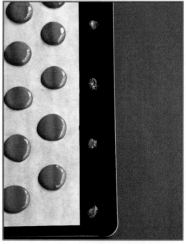

Put some dots of batter on the tray to attach the baking paper.

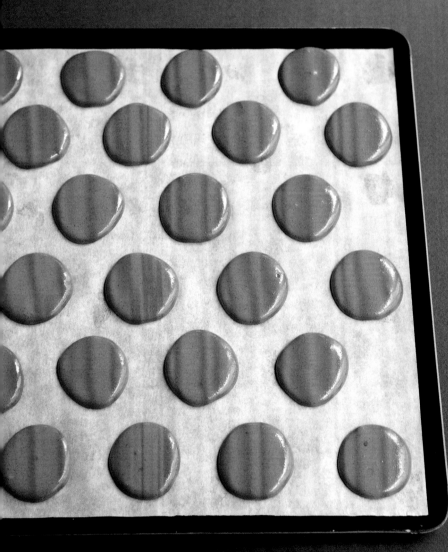

The shells are said to have "crusted" (croûtées) when they are no longer sticky to the touch.

CROÛTAGE (DRYING TIME)

WHAT IS THE DRYING TIME FOR?

THE CROÛTAGE OR drying time creates a thin, dry and resistant film on the surface of the macaron shells. When cooked, it becomes crisp. The moisture in the shell lifts it without cracking the surface, and an even set of "feet" forms around its base.

The drying time can vary by several minutes depending on the temperature of the room. To check whether the shells are ready to be put into the oven, lightly brush the top of one: the batter shouldn't stick to your fingers.

Shell cooked without drying.

Shell cooked after drying time.

COOKING

FOR HOW LONG SHOULD MACARONS BE COOKED?

HERE ARE A few references to be used as guidelines for a fan-forced oven; they can be adjusted according to the type of oven you have by a few degrees or minutes.

MACARON DIAMETER	OVEN TEMPERATURE	COOKING TIME
medium size: 4–6 cm (1½ – 2½ in)	150°C (300°F/Gas 2)	14 minutes
dessert size: 6–8 cm (2½ – 3¼ in)	160°C (315°F/Gas 2–3)	15 minutes
cake base: 16 cm (6¼ in) or more	170°C (325°F/Gas 3)	17 to 18 minutes

STOP COOKING!

WHEN THEY COME out of the oven, slide the baking paper onto a dampened benchtop; this creates a thermal shock that makes the macarons easier to remove.

CHOCOLATE

Chocolate is made from the cocoa bean, the fruit of the cacao tree

COMPOSITION

CHOCOLATE IS A food made from cocoa mass (a mixture of dry cocoa bean extracts and cocoa butter), cocoa butter, pulverised sugar, various amounts of lecithin, and dehydrated milk (in the case of milk chocolate). It also contains fibre, vitamins and minerals that make it an energy food. White chocolate, for its part, doesn't contain any dry cocoa bean extracts, but only cocoa butter, sugar and powdered milk.

The nutritional value of chocolate varies a great deal depending on the variety and brand.

The nutritional information for 100 g (3 1/2 oz) dark chocolate (55–70%):

Carbohydrates .... 54 g (2 oz)	Protein.. 6 g (1/8 oz)
Fats... 27 g (1 oz)	Mineral salts....................................1196.47 mg
Fibre... 9 g (1/4 oz)	**Energy .... 2093–2345 kJ (500–560 cal)**

THE VIRTUES OF CHOCOLATE

FROM A HEALTH POINT OF VIEW, chocolate is a very nutritious food in a very concentrated form. It is high in calcium, phosphate and vitamin D (which promotes the absorption of calcium by the bones).

The main ingredient of chocolate, cocoa, is high in iron, phosphorus, potassium, and vitamins B1 and B9. It can also contain magnesium (known for its calming effect) or else calcium oxalate, which makes dark chocolate harmful for people with liver or rheumatism complaints, or those suffering from obesity.

Finally, chocolate contains vitamin E and, above all, flavonoids — antioxidant substances that are believed to combat ageing and reduce the risk of cardiovascular diseases.

THE DIFFERENTS KINDS OF CHOCOLATE

THE FIRST CRITERION of the quality of chocolate is its cocoa content. The higher the percentage, the less sugar it contains and the more intense its flavour. Make sure you check that the chocolate is a "pure cocoa butter" variety.

For baking, it's best to use a dark chocolate with at least 55% cocoa. Chocolate with a high cocoa percentage (60–75%) gives a deeper flavour. It makes mixtures firmer, in particular ganaches, for which you just need to adjust the quantities of cream and sugar.

Milk chocolate is an excellent chocolate as long as it contains at least 35% cocoa.

Higher in butter and sugar, white chocolate gives a silky texture to ganaches. It is ideal for all flavoured ganaches.

GANACHE

WHAT IS GANACHE?

GANACHE IS A very rich and melt-in-the-mouth preparation made from dark, milk or white chocolate and cream. Used as is or further enhanced by adding a spice, alcohol or flavouring, it is the essential filling of a chocolate macaron.

Ganache can also be flavoured by infusing aromatics (tea, lavender, lemon thyme, cinnamon, citrus zest) in the hot cream. For fruit ganaches, the cream is replaced with a fruit coulis.

THE DIFFERENT GANACHE BASES

Dark chocolate base	Milk chocolate base	White chocolate base
70% chocolate .... 220 g (7³/₄ oz)	Milk chocolate .. 300 g (10¹/₂ oz)	White chocolate .... 400 g (14 oz)
or 55% chocolate..... 250 g (9 oz)	or + dark chocolate 80 g (2³/₄ oz)	Pouring cream ...200 ml (7 fl oz)
Pouring cream .. 200 ml (7 fl oz)	Pouring cream ...200 ml (7 fl oz)	Butter .... 30 g (1 oz)
Butter .... 50 g (1³/₄ oz)	Butter .... 50 g (1³/₄ oz)	

HOW DO YOU MAKE GANACHE?

1. GRATE OR CHOP the chocolate into small pieces so that it melts evenly.
2. Bring the cream to the boil.
3. Pour the hot cream over the chocolate.

Combine using a whisk. Cool a little.
4. When cooled to 40°C (104°F), incorporate the butter, diced. Combine well again so the ganache is smooth.

WHAT CREAM SHOULD I USE WHEN MAKING A GANACHE?

IT IS PREFERABLE to use creams of impeccable bacteriological quality. Sterilised, pasteur- ised or UHT creams are recommended. Choose creams with at least 33% fat.

HOW SHOULD GANACHE BE STORED?

THE SHELF LIFE of ganache is limited to a few days in the refrigerator, because the water content of the cream provides a favour- able environment for the growth of micro- organisms.
Before storing in the refrigerator, cover the ganache with plastic wrap, ensuring it is in contact with the surface of the ganache, to avoid a skin forming.
Some professionals replace the fresh cream with evaporated milk. This extends the shelf life of the ganache, but it doesn't have the same taste or richness as a ganache made with fresh cream.

Panorama of ganaches (milk, dark, white).

BUTTER

Butter is made up of water droplets suspended in butterfat

COMPOSITION

BUTTER IS A 100% natural product, high in vitamin A and carotene.

It is made by churning the cream derived from milk. Twenty litres (700 fl oz) of milk are required to make 1 kg (2 lb 4 oz) of butter. The most common form of butter is made from pasteurised cow's milk.

Raw or farm butter is made exclusively from raw unpasteurised cream. All of its nutritional qualities are therefore preserved and it has a stronger taste, but it doesn't keep as well as pasteurised butter.

Salted butter contains over 5% salt and *demi-sel* (lightly salted) butter 0.5% to 3% salt. Unsalted or "sweet" butter has the lowest salt content.

The nutritional information for 100 g (3 $^{1}/_{2}$ oz) unsalted butter:

Carbohydrates .... 0 g (0 oz)	Water .... 17 g ($^{1}/_{2}$ oz)	Vitamin A .... 710 µg
Protein.................. 0 g (0 oz)	Cholesterol................ 250 mg	Carotene .... 505 µg
Fats *(63% saturated fat)*..........	Calcium...................... 15 mg	**Energy ....3140 kJ (750 cal)**
.... 83 g (3 oz)		

THE ROLES PLAYED BY BUTTER

BUTTER IS MORE easily digested when it is fresh and still in its emulsified form than when it is heated or cooked. In baking, it enhances flavours, and adds richness and creaminess.

Incorporating butter into a cream or ganache also gives it a certain texture that makes it easier to fill the macarons using a piping bag.

Salted butter is suitable for a caramel, and *demi-sel* (lightly salted) butter will enhance the chocolate flavour of certain ganaches. Given its high fat content, it should nevertheless be used sparingly.

Did you know? While butter has been known since ancient times, it became an important dietary and economic staple during the Middle Ages. It was then one of the only sources of fat, a "poor-man's fat", more readily available than oil and less expensive than lard.

The colour of butter varies from a pale to a dark yellow and depends on the diet of the cows, which varies according to the season, climate and pasture.

BUTTER: A USER'S GUIDE

WHICH BUTTER SHOULD I USE?

For baking, it is recommended you use butter with an 82% fat content, the one most commonly available in stores, and to avoid margarine or reduced-fat butters.

While *demi-sel* (lightly salted) butter lifts an apple tart or intensifies the flavour of chocolate, salted butter, for its part, will work perfectly in a caramel sauce.

HOW DO YOU STORE BUTTER?

Butter has a limited shelf life. It oxidises when exposed to air, and light and heat breaks down its components. It can then become rancid and develop an unpleasant taste and smell.

It is therefore preferable to store butter in the refrigerator, well wrapped and protected from air and light, for up to 8 weeks for pasteurised butter and only 3 to 4 weeks for raw butter.

Salted and *demi-sel* (lightly salted) butter keep for a longer time than unsalted butter thanks to the presence of salt, a natural preservative.

WHAT IS CRÈME MOUSSELINE?

Crème mousseline is a crème pâtissière or pastry cream to which a certain amount of softened butter is added once it has cooked and cooled a little. This gives it creaminess, but also makes it more solid when cold. It will thus join the macaron shells together evenly and without oozing out.

With added flavours (rosewater, orange flower water, etc.) or just vanilla, it is ideal for macarons with fresh fruit and has the advantage of being lighter and not as rich as butter cream.

It's important, however, not to fill macarons with *crème mousseline* too far ahead of time, because *crème mousseline* is moister than butter cream and tends to soften the shells quickly. It is therefore strongly recommended that you fill and assemble the macarons not long before serving them.

WHAT IS GANACHE?

Ganache is a mixture of cream (or milk, or even fruit coulis) and chocolate, in almost equal quantities (see page 38). The addition of butter to a ganache makes it more "melting" in the mouth. Add a few small knobs of butter once the ganache mixture is quite smooth and allow to cool before filling the macarons.

HOW DO YOU MAKE SALTED-BUTTER CARAMEL?

Pour the sugar into a saucepan. As soon as it turns a lovely caramel colour, pour in the cream (watch out for spatters), dissolve the mixture on a gentle heat and bind with salted butter off the heat. Allow to cool before filling the macarons.

BUTTER CREAM

THE CLASSIC RECIPE

A CLASSIC BUTTER cream is made from egg yolks and sugar syrup or meringue, which are incorporated into softened butter.

Butter cream is very rich, and therefore tends to be used more to fill sponge cakes or a génoise (mocha sponge, swiss roll), which have a lighter texture than a macaron.

Flavoured with an extract or other flavouring, butter cream can be used to join macaron shells. It is important, however, not to overfill the shells.

A LIGHTER RECIPE FOR MACARONS:
ALMOND BUTTER CREAM

BEAT THE SOFTENED butter vigorously in a mixing bowl using a whisk until it is quite soft and smooth.

At this stage, add the icing sugar and whisk again to cream the butter. Finally, incorporate the ground almonds and continue to whisk well to aerate and give lightness to the cream.

Flavour the cream depending on the flavour of the macarons, with an extract, flavouring or fruit liqueur.

Creaming the butter.

Ready-to-use butter cream.

FRUIT FILLINGS

HOW DO YOU FILL MACARONS WITH FRESH FRUIT?

REDCURRANTS, BLUEBERRIES, BLACKCURRANTS, raspberries or finely diced fresh fruit can be jellied in a coulis or attached to the macaron shells at the last minute with a dab of ganache, *crème mousseline* or chantilly cream.

CAN YOU MAKE FRUIT GANACHES?

YES, ALL OR part of the cream is replaced with fruit coulis or pulp.

Traditional ganaches can be flavoured by incorporating small pieces of fresh, freeze-dried, crystallised or candied fruit. The addition of a liqueur, essential oil (edible) or fruit flavouring will also flavour a chocolate ganache.

WHAT IS A MARMALADE?

MARMALADE IS ORIGINALLY a very thick mixture made using macerated citrus fruits cooked with sugar. The natural pectin contained in the fruits gives it its jelly-like consistency.

The marmalades used to fill macarons can be made using fresh or frozen fruit. Whole, chopped or puréed fruit is cooked for less time and with less sugar than a jam in order to preserve its texture and acidity. In most cases, depending on the fruit, some sort of gelling agent needs to be added to compensate for the shorter cooking time and lower sugar content.

CAN READY-MADE JAMS BE USED?

YES, YOU CAN use jams that don't contain very large pieces of fruit. Since it is very sweet, these jams are just used as a "dab of glue" for joining shells, or they may be combined with finely diced fresh or dried fruit.

CAN PECTIN OR AGAR-AGAR
BE USED INSTEAD OF GELATINE?

PECTIN IS A plant-based substance. It is sold in stores in powdered form. Adding pectin allows you to reduce the amount of sugar and gel fruits more quickly.

Agar-agar has more gelling power and is a good substitute for pectin or gelatine. It results in a better release of flavours in the mouth.

Allow 1 level teaspoon of powdered agar-agar for 500 ml (17 fl oz) of liquid, depending on the fruit used and the desired consistency.

Unlike gelatine, which dissolves when heated, agar-agar needs to be diluted in a cold liquid or coulis, and then heated to 85°C (185°F).

CUSTOMISATION

How to personalise your macarons and give them a festive touch …

COLOURED SUGAR ON FILLED MACARONS

For about 15 macarons
Caster sugar...................... 220 g (7 ³/₄ oz)

Glucose syrup .... 80 g (2 ³/₄ oz)
Colouring (powder, paste or liquid)

1. Bring 80 ml (2¹/₂ fl oz) water, sugar, glucose and a little colouring to the boil. Without stirring, bring the syrup to a maximum temperature of 120°C (250°F).
2. Line a baking tray with baking paper or a silicone mat.

3. Stop the cooking of the sugar at 120°C (250°F) and wait for 2 minutes. Dip half the macarons in the syrup (be careful not to burn yourself!). Arrange them on the tray.

CHOCOLATE COATING ON FILLED MACARONS *(not pictured)*

For about 20 macarons
Lollipop sticks 20

Chocolate (bits, buttons or
broken up) .... 600 g (1 lb 5 oz)

1. Once the shells are cooked, turn them over on a tray. Fill half of them with a small knob of chocolate ganache (see recipe pages 66–69), then push the lollipop sticks lightly into the ganache. Cover with the remaining shells and press lightly to hold the lollipop sticks in place. Place in the refrigerator for 30 minutes.
2. Melt 400 g (14 oz) of the chocolate in a bowl set over a saucepan of simmering water. Once it is completely melted (40–45°C/105–115°F), remove from the saucepan and incorporate the remaining chocolate to lower the temperature of the mixture. Mix well so that all the solids have dissolved, then place the bowl back

over the saucepan for a minute just to bring it back to the right temperature (30–33°C/85–90°F).
  This technique, called "tempering" the chocolate, preserves its glossiness and avoids streaks of cocoa butter once it cools down.
3. Dip the macarons into the melted chocolate with the help of the lollipop sticks. Hold over the mixing bowl to let the excess run off then carefully arrange the macarons on a tray covered with a silicone mat, a dipping sheet *(feuille guitare)* or plastic wrap. Carefully remove the lollipop sticks. Place in the refrigerator to set.

PAINTING THE SHELLS AFTER COOKING *(not pictured)*

A simple and quick technique for customising the shells after cooking, using ingredients ready to hand: you just need to lightly dip a pastry brush into a little of the uncooked batter left in the mixing bowl,

some pistachio paste or a little ganache or butter cream. Lightly brush the shells using clean but delicate strokes, in order to create stripes, then let the shells dry at room temperature.

CUSTOMISATION *(continued)*

DRIZZLED CHOCOLATE *(on filled macarons)*

For about 20 macarons
Dark chocolate.................. 125 g (4 ¹/₂ oz)

Canola oil (or other neutrally flavoured oil) ....1 teaspoon

1. Melt the dark chocolate with the oil, using a double boiler or in a microwave oven.

2. Cut out a 20 × 30 cm (8 × 12 in) piece of baking paper. Roll it up on itself, making a cone and turn the ends inside. Half-fill with melted chocolate then, after folding in the ends, snip a small hole in the tip.

3. With a sharp back-and-forth movement, drizzle thin threads of chocolate over the top of the macarons. Place in the refrigerator for a few minutes to set the chocolate.

EDIBLE SHIMMER POWDER, AND GOLD AND SILVER LEAF *(after cooking)*

Once the shells have cooled and been removed from the baking paper, make some of them up with edible shimmer powder, using a small brush to give them shiny and sparkly highlights.
There is quite an extensive range of shades available at cake decorating stockists these days (copper, ivory, bronze, silver, frost …), which allows you to customise macarons that are the same colour by giving them different highlights.
Gold or silver leaf is extremely thin and volatile: it needs to be placed on the shells with great care using a small brush.

STARDUST *(before cooking)*

After you have piped the macarons on the baking tray, dip a toothbrush into some (liquid) colouring, then flick the bristles over the macarons.

BISCUIT CRUMBS *(before cooking)*

Process some tea biscuits or some *pain d'épices* (French gingerbread) that have been dried out in the oven (20–30 minutes at 150°C (300°F/Gas 2) depending on how thick the pieces are).
After piping the macarons onto the baking tray, dust with crumbs using a fine strainer.
Tap lightly on the bottom of the trays so the excess crumbs fall off.

OTHER FANCY TOUCHES *(before cooking)*

Small sugar pearls or balls, crystallised flowers, flavoured sugars, gold or silver flakes: all of these decorations need to be placed on the macaron shells very gently, just before putting in the oven. Be careful not to push too hard, because some of them could pierce the shells and prevent them from rising.

From top to bottom: drizzled chocolate, shimmer powder, stardust.

ANY OTHER QUESTIONS?

Answers to all the other questions

HOW DO I STORE AND KEEP MACARONS?

To GET THE most out of the taste and texture of macarons, it's advisable to let them spend 1 night in the refrigerator in an airtight container, so that all their flavours can develop. Keep in the container in the refrigerator for a maximum of 2 to 3 days.

CAN MACARONS BE MADE FAR AHEAD OF TIME?

IF YOU WOULD like to make the macarons in advance, you just need to keep them, carefully packed, in an airtight container in the freezer. You then just have to place them in the refrigerator, in their container, overnight to allow them to return to the right temperature. You will, however, need to eat them within 24 hours.

WHY ARE MY MACARONS CRACKED?

THERE ARE SEVERAL possible reasons …
· The temperature of the oven is too high: the shells rise up too quickly, like a soufflé, and crack. Don't hesitate to monitor the first few minutes of cooking and to open the oven door to drop the temperature by a few degrees.
· Insufficient working (*macaronage*) of the batter: if the meringue isn't worked with the almonds enough, the batter will be too foamy and aerated. When cooked, it will react in the oven like a cake or soufflé.
· The shells haven't formed enough of a crust: the drying time (*croûtage*) creates a film on top that assists the cooking. The shells "seal" more quickly and keep the moisture inside, which prevents them from cracking.
· Too many trays in the oven: it is important to leave a certain amount of space between each tray to allow the heat to circulate properly and cook the shells evenly. An overloaded oven will lower the temperature, and the humidity generated by the shells cooking runs the risk of softening them.

WHY ARE MY SHELLS FLAT,
WITHOUT ANY PRETTY "FEET"?

THE BATTER HAS had too much *macaronage*: it is too runny because it has been overworked. The egg whites are "broken" and no longer rise when cooked.

WHY AREN'T MY SHELLS NICE AND ROUND?

· THE PIPING WASN'T steady.
· The trays are not completely flat.

· The baking paper is creased or wrinkled and the batter has gone out of shape.

WHY AREN'T MY SHELLS NICE AND SMOOTH?

· THE TANT POUR tant wasn't finely mixed or sifted enough.

· The batter wasn't worked for long enough.

WHY IS IT HARD TO REMOVE THE SHELLS
FROM THE BAKING PAPER?

· THE SHELLS HAVE not been cooked for long enough.
· The shells have been removed too quickly. When they come out of the oven, it's important to slide the baking paper onto a dampened benchtop: this creates a thermal shock that allows the macarons to be detached more easily.

WHY HAVE MY SHELLS CHANGED COLOUR IN THE OVEN?

BE CAREFUL IF using pale colours! Plain macarons, as well as light-coloured ones, tend to darken or brown during their cooking time.

So, don't hesitate to lower the temperature of the oven just a little bit and increase the cooking time by a few minutes so the colour isn't affected.

CHAPTER 2

CLASSIC
MACARONS

There are two schools of thought when it comes to making macarons: one where the sugar is incorporated into the meringue cold and one where the sugar is cooked. I recommend the latter for these macarons with must-try flavours.

PLAIN

A contrast between two textures:
crisp on the outside and soft on the inside

MEMO

- For 40 macarons 3 cm (1¹/₄ in) in diameter
- Preparation time.............. 50 minutes
- Drying time..................... 30 minutes
- Cooking time.................... 14 minutes
- Refrigeration time .... 1 hour
- Oven temperature .. 150°C (300°F/Gas 2)

INGREDIENTS

- Ground almonds...............200 g (7 oz)
- Icing sugar ....200 g (7 oz)
- Water .... 75 ml (2¹/₂ fl oz)
- Caster sugar.....................200 g (7 oz)
- Egg whites........... 2 × 80 g (2 × 2³/₄ oz)
- Vanilla bean...................................... 1
- White colouring (optional, see page 24)

Almond butter cream
- Softened butter...250 g (9 oz)
- Icing sugar..140 g (5 oz)
- Ground almonds ....160 g (5³/₄ oz)

STRUCTURE

A natural meringue colour, the shells are partnered with the richness of an almond butter cream for an authentic taste.

Pipe a knob of butter cream on half the macaron shells.

THE MACARONS

1. Process then carefully sift the ground almonds and icing sugar (this is called the *tant pour tant*: see pages 12–13). Set aside.

2. In a saucepan, bring the water and caster sugar to the boil. Without stirring, make sure the temperature of the resulting syrup doesn't go above 115°C (240°F).

3. Gently beat 80 g (2³/₄ oz) egg whites to soft peaks, then increase the speed of the beater when the temperature of the syrup passes 105°C (220°F). When the syrup reaches 115°C (240°F) remove the saucepan from the heat and pour the syrup in a thin stream into the beaten egg whites. Continue to beat the meringue for about 10 minutes, so that it cools.

4. Combine the *tant pour tant* and the remaining unbeaten egg whites, making a smooth almond paste.

5. Scrape the vanilla bean and incorporate a few vanilla seeds into the almond paste, then add the colouring (if desired).

6. Using a flexible spatula, incorporate about a third of the meringue into the almond paste to loosen the mixture a little, then add the rest of the meringue, working the batter carefully.

7. Fill a piping bag fitted with an 8 mm (³/₈ in) nozzle with batter. Attach a sheet of baking paper to each baking tray, placing small dots of batter in each corner. Pipe out small, regular and well-spaced rounds, each about the size of a walnut. Lightly tap the bottom of the trays and allow the macarons to form a crust at room temperature for 30 minutes.

8. Preheat the oven to 150°C (300°F/Gas 2).

9. Bake in the oven for 14 minutes. When you take them out, carefully place the baking paper on a dampened benchtop: the shells will be easier to remove.

THE BUTTER CREAM

1. Beat the softened butter vigorously using a whisk or electric beater, to give it a smooth and creamy texture. Add the icing sugar and beat again.

2. Finally, incorporate the ground almonds and whisk again for a few minutes to aerate the cream and give it lightness.

THE ASSEMBLY

Using a piping bag fitted with an 8 mm (³/₈ in) nozzle, generously fill half the shells with butter cream, then assemble the macarons with the remaining shells. Place the macarons in the refrigerator for an hour.

VANILLA

Smooth shells
A brilliant white
A delicate flavour of vanilla

MEMO

- For 40 macarons 3 cm (1¹/₄ in) in diameter
- Preparation time............... 50 minutes
- Drying time...................... 30 minutes
- Cooking time.................... 14 minutes
- Refrigeration time .... 1 to 1¹/₂ hrs
- Oven temperature .. 150°C (300°F/Gas 2)

INGREDIENTS

- Ground almonds...............200 g (7 oz)
- Icing sugar ....200 g (7 oz)
- Water....................... 75 ml (2¹/₂ fl oz)
- Caster sugar......................200 g (7 oz)
- Egg whites............ 2 × 80 g (2 × 2³/₄ oz)
- Vanilla bean................................. ¹/₂
- White colouring (optional, see page 24)

VANILLA BUTTER CREAM

- Softened butter 250 g (9 oz)
- Icing sugar ...... 140 g (5 oz)
- Ground almonds...............
  ....160 g (5³/₄ oz)
- Vanilla bean............¹/₂ (or a few drops of vanilla extract)

CHANTILLY CREAM WITH MASCARPONE

- Mascarpone..... 250 g (9 oz)
- Icing sugar .... 60 g (2¹/₄ oz)
- Vanilla bean.............¹/₂ (or a few drops vanilla extract)
- Pouring cream ....
  .... 250 ml (9 fl oz)

VANILLA CRÈME MOUSSELINE

- Milk..........500 ml (17 fl oz)
- Vanilla bean................... ¹/₂
- Egg yolks........................ 6
- Sugar .... 125 g (4¹/₂ oz)
- Flour .... 20 g (³/₄ oz)
- Cornflour.......... 30 g (1 oz)
- Butter ....100 g (3¹/₂ oz)

From top to bottom: vanilla butter cream,
chantilly cream with mascarpone, vanilla crème mousseline.

THE MACARONS

1. Process then carefully sift the *tant pour tant* (see pages 12–13). Set aside.

2. In a saucepan, bring the water and caster sugar to the boil. Without stirring, make sure the temperature of the resulting syrup doesn't go above 115°C (240°F).

3. Gently beat 80 g (2³/₄ oz) egg whites to soft peaks, then increase the beater speed once the temperature of the syrup passes 105°C (220°F). When the syrup reaches 115°C (240°F) remove the saucepan from the heat and pour the syrup in a thin stream into the beaten egg whites. Continue to beat the meringue for about 10 minutes, so that it cools a little.

4. Combine the *tant pour tant* with the remaining egg whites, making a smooth almond paste. Scrape the half vanilla bean and incorporate a few vanilla seeds, then add the white colouring (if desired).

5. Using a flexible spatula, incorporate about a third of the meringue into the almond paste in order to loosen the mixture a little, then add the rest of the meringue, working the batter.

6. Fill a piping bag fitted with an 8 mm (³/₈ in) nozzle with batter. Attach a sheet of baking paper to each baking tray by placing small dots of batter in the corners. Pipe out small, regular and well-spaced rounds, about the size of a walnut. Lightly tap the bottom of the trays and allow the macarons to form a crust at room temperature for 30 minutes.

7. Preheat the oven to 150°C (300°F/Gas 2). Bake for 14 minutes then place the baking paper on a dampened benchtop: the shells will be easier to remove.

A SELECTION OF FILLINGS

Vanilla butter cream: make a plain butter cream, (see method page 57). Scrape the half vanilla bean and incorporate the seeds, or add a few drops of vanilla extract.

Chantilly cream with mascarpone: combine the mascarpone, icing sugar and vanilla seeds or vanilla extract so that you have a very smooth cream. Whip the well chilled pouring cream manually or using an electric beater. Halfway through the process, incorporate the mascarpone mixture and beat again until you obtain quite a thick chantilly.

Vanilla crème mousseline: heat the milk over a gentle heat with the half vanilla bean. Beat the egg yolks and sugar, then add the flour and cornflour and beat again. Pour the hot milk over this mixture then return the combined preparation to a gentle heat for 3 to 4 minutes, continually stirring, until it thickens. Remove it from the heat and thoroughly mix in the butter (cut into small pieces). Decant the cream into an airtight container then set it aside for at least 90 minutes in the refrigerator.

THE ASSEMBLY

Using a piping bag fitted with an 8 mm (³/₈ in) nozzle, fill half the macaron shells with your choice of filling then assemble the macarons with the remaining shells. Place the macarons in the refrigerator for an hour if they are filled with butter cream; otherwise, keep them in an airtight container.

PISTACHIO

*Whether as a fine paste, roughly crushed or concentrated
in an essence, the pistachio will bring its sweet flavour to the
cream or ganache you choose to fill your macarons*

MEMO

- For 40 macarons 3 cm (1¹/₄ in) in diameter
- Preparation time.............. 50 minutes
- Drying time...................... 30 minutes
- Cooking time................... 14 minutes
- Refrigeration time .... 1 hour
- Oven temperature .. 150°C (300°F/Gas 2)

INGREDIENTS

- Ground almonds...............200 g (7 oz)
- Icing sugar ....200 g (7 oz)
- Water........................ 75 ml (2¹/₂ fl oz)
- Caster sugar......................200 g (7 oz)
- Egg whites............ 2 × 80 g (2 × 2³/₄ oz)
- Green and yellow colouring

PISTACHIO BUTTER CREAM

- Softened butter 250 g (9 oz)
- Icing sugar ....25 g (1 oz)
- Ground almonds.............. ....70 g (2¹/₂ oz)
- Pistachio paste .... (see below).... 80 g (2³/₄ oz)

PISTACHIO MASCARPONE CREAM

- Mascarpone... 400 g (14 oz)
- Icing sugar .... 80 g (2³/₄ oz)
- Pouring cream .... 200 ml (7 fl oz)
- Unsalted shelled pistachios .... 90 g (3¹/₄ oz)

PISTACHIO CHOCOLATE GANACHE

- White chocolate .... 400 g (14 oz)
- Pouring cream .... 200 ml (7 fl oz)
- Pistachio paste .... (see below).... 60 g (2¹/₄ oz)

HOW TO MAKE PISTACHIO PASTE

*Grind shelled unsalted pistachios very finely in a food processor, with a little orgeat or sugar
syrup (see glossary), until you have a thick paste. You can also add a drop of green
colouring. Allow 1 tablespoon of syrup for 100 g (3¹/₂ oz) pistachios.*

From top to bottom: pistachio butter cream,
pistachio mascarpone cream, pistachio chocolate ganache.

THE MACARONS

1. Process then carefully sift the *tant pour tant* (see pages 12–13). Set aside.

2. In a saucepan, bring the water and caster sugar to the boil. Without stirring, make sure the temperature of the resulting syrup doesn't go above 115°C (240°F).

3. Gently beat 80 g (2³/₄ oz) egg whites to soft peaks, then increase the beater speed once the temperature of the syrup passes 105°C (220°F). When the syrup reaches 115°C (240°F) remove the saucepan from the heat and pour the syrup in a thin stream into the beaten egg whites. Continue to beat the meringue for about 10 minutes, so that it cools a little.

4. Combine the *tant pour tant* with the remaining egg whites, making a smooth almond paste. Add 2 to 3 drops of green colouring and a drop of yellow colouring, to create something like a pistachio colour.

5. Using a flexible spatula, incorporate about a third of the meringue into the almond paste in order to loosen the mixture a little, then add the rest of the meringue, carefully working the batter.

6. Fill a piping bag fitted with an 8 mm (³/₈ in) nozzle with batter. Attach a sheet of baking paper to each baking tray by placing small dots of batter in the corners. Pipe out small, regular and well-spaced rounds. Lightly tap the bottom of the trays and allow the macarons to form a crust at room temperature for 30 minutes.

7. Preheat the oven to 150°C (300°F/Gas 2).

8. Cook in the oven for 14 minutes. As soon as they come out of the oven, carefully place the baking paper on a dampened benchtop: the shells will be easier to remove.

A SELECTION OF FILLINGS

Pistachio butter cream: beat the softened butter using a whisk or an electric beater, to obtain a smooth and creamy texture. Add the icing sugar and beat again. Finally, incorporate the ground almonds and pistachio paste, then beat again for a few minutes to aerate the cream and give it lightness.

Pistachio mascarpone cream: combine the mascarpone with the icing sugar to make a smooth cream. Whip the well-chilled pouring cream. Halfway through the process, incorporate the mascarpone mixture and beat until you have a thick cream. Incorporate the pistachios, roughly chopped with a knife or coarsely ground in the food processor.

Pistachio chocolate ganache: break up the chocolate into a mixing bowl. Heat the pouring cream and the pistachio paste in a saucepan. Pour this mixture over the chocolate. Mix well to dissolve the solids and smooth out the ganache. Allow to cool to room temperature, then chill for at least 1 hour before filling the macarons (even better if made the day before).

THE ASSEMBLY

Using a piping bag fitted with an 8 mm (³/₈ in) nozzle, fill half the macaron shells with the filling of your choice, then assemble the macarons with the remaining shells. Place the macarons in the refrigerator for an hour.

CHOCOLATE

A subtle blend of almonds and cocoa to naturally colour the shells
Chocolate three ways: crisp, soft and melting

MEMO

- For 40 macarons 3 cm (1¹/₄ in) in diameter
- Preparation time............... 50 minutes
- Drying time..................... 30 minutes
- Cooking time.................... 14 minutes
- Refrigeration time ..... 1 hour or 1 night
- Oven temperature 150°C (300°F/Gas 2)

INGREDIENTS

- Ground almonds........... 180 g (6¹/₄ oz)
- Icing sugar .... 200 g (7 oz)
- Cocoa powder .... 30 g (1 oz)
- Water........................ 75 ml (2¹/₂ fl oz)
- Caster sugar .... 200 g (7 oz)
- Egg whites .... 2 × 80 g (2 × 2³/₄ oz)
- Brown colouring (optional)

Chocolate ganache

- Dark chocolate 55–70% ....250–220 g (9 – 7³/₄ oz)
- Pouring cream ....200 ml (7 fl oz)
- Sugar .... 10–20 g (¹/₄ – ³/₄ oz)
  (depending on the chocolate used)
- Butter .... 50 g (1³/₄ oz)
- Coffee extract (optional)..2 drops

STRUCTURE

An almost 100% chocolate macaron.
A dark chocolate ganache that may be more or less intense, depending on taste.

THE MACARONS

1. Process then carefully sift the *tant pour tant* (see pages 12–13) and the cocoa. Set aside.

2. In a saucepan, bring the water and caster sugar to the boil. Without stirring, make sure the temperature of the resulting syrup doesn't go above 115°C (240°F).

3. Gently beat 80 g (2³/₄ oz) egg whites to soft peaks, then increase the beater speed once the temperature of the syrup passes 105°C (220°F). When the syrup reaches 115°C (240°F) remove the saucepan from the heat and pour the syrup in a thin stream into the beaten egg whites. Continue to beat the meringue for about 10 minutes, so that it cools a little.

4. Combine the *tant pour tant* and the cocoa with the remaining egg whites, making a smooth paste. Add a little brown colouring for a stronger colour if desired.

5. Using a flexible spatula, incorporate about a third of the meringue into the almond paste in order to loosen the mixture a little, then add the rest of the meringue, carefully working the batter.

6. Fill a piping bag fitted with an 8 mm (³/₈ in) nozzle with batter. Attach a sheet of baking paper to each baking tray by placing small dots of batter in the corners. Pipe small, regular and well-spaced rounds about the size of a walnut. Lightly tap the bottom of the trays and allow the macarons to form a crust at room temperature for 30 minutes.

7. Preheat the oven to 150°C (300°F/Gas 2).

8. Bake in the oven for 14 minutes. When they come out of the oven, carefully place the baking paper on a dampened benchtop: the shells will be easier to remove.

THE CHOCOLATE GANACHE

1. Break the chocolate up in pieces into a mixing bowl.

2. Heat the cream and the sugar in a saucepan over a medium heat.

3. Pour the hot cream over the chocolate and gently combine to dissolve the chocolate.

4. Finally incorporate the butter, cut into small pieces, and the coffee extract. Combine well so that the ganache is smooth.

5. Allow to cool to room temperature, then place in the refrigerator for at least 1 hour before filling the macarons (even better if made the day before).

THE ASSEMBLY

Using a piping bag fitted with an 8 mm (³/₈ in) nozzle, fill half the macaron shells with chocolate ganache then assemble the macarons with the remaining shells. Place the macarons in the refrigerator for an hour.

COFFEE

Shells flavoured and coloured with coffee extract
A mocha treat that's both crisp and melting

MEMO

- For 40 macarons 3 cm (1¹/₄ in) in diameter
- Preparation time.............. 50 minutes
- Drying time..................... 30 minutes
- Cooking time................... 14 minutes
- Oven temperature .. 150°C (300°F/Gas 2)

INGREDIENTS

- Ground almonds...............200 g (7 oz)
- Icing sugar ....200 g (7 oz)
- Water .... 75 ml (2¹/₂ fl oz)
- Caster sugar.....................200 g (7 oz)
- Egg whites............ 2 × 80 g (2 × 2³/₄ oz)
- Liquid coffee extract

COFFEE CREAM

- Softened butter.................250 g (9 oz)
- Icing sugar .... 140 g (5 oz)
- Ground almonds.......... 160 g (5 ³/₄ oz)
- Coffee extract ....1–2 drops
  (or 20 g/³/₄ oz instant coffee)

COFFEE JELLY

- Gelatine ....6 sheets
- Good coffee .... 500 ml (17 fl oz)
- Caster sugar................... 40 g (1¹/₂ oz)
- Coffee or vanilla extract..........3 drops
  (or 2 pieces orange zest)

STRUCTURE

Butter cream providing a creamy texture and joining the shells together well.
Coffee jelly, a lighter option, adding freshness to the crispness of the macaron.

Using a small cookie-cutter, cut out rounds of jelly.

THE MACARONS

1. Process then carefully sift the *tant pour tant* (see pages 12–13). Set aside.
2. In a saucepan, bring the water and caster sugar to the boil. Without stirring, make sure the temperature of the resulting syrup doesn't go above 115°C (240°F).
3. Gently beat 80 g (2³/₄ oz) egg whites to soft peaks, then increase the beater speed once the temperature of the syrup passes 105°C (220°F). When the syrup reaches 115°C (240°F) remove the saucepan from the heat and pour the syrup in a thin stream into the beaten egg whites. Continue to beat the meringue for about 10 minutes so that it cools a little.
4. Combine the *tant pour tant* with the remaining egg whites, making a smooth almond paste. Add a few drops of coffee extract and combine.
5. Using a flexible spatula, incorporate about a third of the meringue into the almond paste in order to loosen the mixture a little, then add the rest of the meringue, carefully working the batter.
6. Fill a piping bag fitted with an 8 mm (³/₈ in) nozzle with batter. Attach a sheet of baking paper to each baking tray by placing small dots of batter in the corners. Pipe small, regular and well-spaced rounds about the size of a walnut. Lightly tap the bottom of the trays and allow the macarons to form a crust at room temperature for 30 minutes.
7. Preheat the oven to 150°C (300°F/Gas 2). Bake for 14 minutes then place the baking paper on a dampened benchtop: the shells will be easier to remove.

A SELECTION OF FILLINGS

Coffee cream: make a butter cream, (see method page 57). Incorporate a few drops of coffee extract or the instant coffee dissolved in 1 tablespoon hot water. Fill half the macaron shells with coffee cream then assemble the macarons with the remaining shells.
Coffee jelly: soak the gelatine sheets in a bowl of cold water to soften them. Heat the coffee and the sugar. Add the coffee or vanilla extract, or infuse the orange zest. Squeeze out the gelatine sheets then add them to the coffee, stirring to dissolve them completely into the mixture. Pour the whole mixture into a tray in a layer 1 cm (¹/₂ in) thick, and place in the freezer for at least 2 hours to set. Unmould the jelly onto a sheet of baking paper and allow to thaw for 30 minutes at room temperature. Thirty minutes before serving, cut out small rounds of jelly using a plain 2 or 3 cm (³/₄ or 1¹/₄ in) cookie-cutter then join the macarons just before serving them.

CARAMEL

Like a caramel bonbon
Crisp and melting, but it doesn't stick to your teeth!

MEMO

- For 40 macarons 3 cm (1¹/₄ in) in diameter
- Preparation time............... 50 minutes
- Drying time...................... 30 minutes
- Cooking time.................... 14 minutes
- Refrigeration time .... 2¹/₂ hours
- Oven temperature .. 150°C (300°F/Gas 2)

INGREDIENTS

- Ground almonds...............200 g (7 oz)
- Icing sugar ....200 g (7 oz)
- Water........................ 75 ml (2¹/₂ fl oz)
- Caster sugar......................200 g (7 oz)
- Egg whites............ 2 × 80 g (2 × 2³/₄ oz)
- Caramel or light-brown colouring (or a few drops of coffee extract + 2 drops of yellow colouring)

Salted-butter caramel
- Caster sugar.. 250 g (9 oz)
- Water ....75 ml (2¹/₂ fl oz)
- Fresh full-fat pouring cream .... 120 ml (4 fl oz)
- Salted butter.. 200 g (7 oz)

STRUCTURE

A lightly golden shell.
A rich caramel with cream and butter.

Carefully pour the cream into the caramel.

THE MACARONS

1. Process then carefully sift the *tant pour tant* (see pages 12–13). Set aside.
2. In a saucepan, bring the water and caster sugar to the boil. Without stirring, make sure the temperature of the resulting syrup doesn't go above 115°C (240°F).
3. Gently beat 80 g (2¾ oz) egg whites to soft peaks, then increase the beater speed once the temperature of the syrup passes 105°C (220°F). When the syrup reaches 115°C (240°F) remove the saucepan from the heat and pour the syrup in a thin stream into the beaten egg whites. Continue to beat the meringue for about 10 minutes, so that it cools a little.
4. Combine the *tant pour tant* with the remaining egg whites, making a smooth almond paste. Add the colourings and/or the coffee extract to create a pale caramel colour.
5. Using a flexible spatula, incorporate about a third of the meringue into the almond paste in order to loosen the mixture a little, then add the rest of the meringue, carefully working the batter.
6. Fill a piping bag fitted with an 8 mm (³/₈ in) nozzle with batter. Attach a sheet of baking paper to each baking tray by placing some dots of batter in the corners. Pipe out small, regular and well-spaced rounds about the size of a walnut. Lightly tap the bottom of the trays and allow the macarons to form a crust at room temperature for 30 minutes.
7. Preheat the oven to 150°C (300°F/Gas 2).
8. Bake in the oven for 14 minutes. When they come out of the oven, carefully place the baking paper on a dampened benchtop: the shells will be easier to remove.

THE SALTED-BUTTER CARAMEL

1. Heat the sugar and water in a saucepan, over a medium heat. Without stirring too much, watch over the sugar until it becomes a lovely light-brown caramel colour.
2. Next add the pouring cream, little by little, gently stirring with a spatula to stop the caramel cooking any further. Watch out for spatters! The caramel will foam up and can burn.
3. Once the cream is well incorporated into the caramel, put in the thermometer and monitor the temperature. Once it reaches 108°C (226°F), remove from the heat and incorporate the butter in small pieces. Beat or whisk until the caramel is smooth and even.
4. Pour into a suitable container and chill in the refrigerator for at least 1½ hours so that the caramel thickens.

THE ASSEMBLY

Using a piping bag fitted with an 8 mm (³/₈ in) nozzle, fill half the macaron shells with salted-butter caramel, then assemble the macarons with the remaining shells. Place the macarons in the refrigerator for an hour.

STRAWBERRY

A stunning contrast of textures and flavours:
the tartness of the strawberry, the creaminess of the
chocolate and the crispness of the macaron

MEMO

- For 40 macarons 3 cm (1¹/₄ in) in diameter
- Preparation time............... 50 minutes
- Drying time...................... 30 minutes
- Cooking time.................... 14 minutes
- Refrigeration time ....1 night + 1 hour
- Oven temperature .. 150°C (300°F/Gas 2)

INGREDIENTS

- Ground almonds...............200 g (7 oz)
- Icing sugar ....200 g (7 oz)
- Water ....75 ml (2 ¹/₂ fl oz)
- Caster sugar.....................200 g (7 oz)
- Egg whites............ 2 × 80 g (2 × 2³/₄ oz)
- Red colouring

Strawberry ganache (make the day before)
- Strawberries...300 g (10¹/₂ oz)
- Caster sugar...25 g (1 oz)
- White chocolate .... 200 g (7 oz)
- Milk chocolate ....100 g (3¹/₂ oz)

STRUCTURE

Shells coloured a pretty pink.
A mildly chocolatey ganache flavoured with strawberry coulis.

Strain the hot coulis over the chocolate.

THE MACARONS

1. Process then carefully sift the *tant pour tant* (see pages 12–13). Set aside.
2. In a saucepan, bring the water and caster sugar to the boil. Without stirring, make sure the temperature of the resulting syrup doesn't go above 115°C (240°F).
3. Gently beat 80 g (2³/₄ oz) egg whites to soft peaks, then increase the beater speed once the temperature of the syrup passes 105°C (220°F). When the syrup reaches 115°C (240°F) remove the saucepan from the heat and pour the syrup in a thin stream into the beaten egg whites. Continue to beat the meringue for about 10 minutes, so that it cools down a little.
4. Combine the *tant pour tant* with the remaining egg whites, making a smooth almond paste. Add one or two drops of red colouring, for a more or less intense colour according to preference.
5. Using a flexible spatula, incorporate about a third of the meringue into the almond paste in order to loosen the mixture a little, then add the rest of the meringue, carefully working the batter.
6. Fill a piping bag fitted with an 8 mm (³/₈ in) nozzle with batter. Attach the baking paper to each baking tray by placing small dots of batter in the corners. Pipe out small, regular and well-spaced rounds, about the size of a walnut. Lightly tap the bottom of the trays and allow them to form a crust at room temperature for 30 minutes.
7. Preheat the oven to 150°C (300°F/Gas 2).
8. Bake in the oven for 14 minutes. When they come out of the oven, gently place the baking paper on a dampened benchtop: the shells will be easier to remove.

THE STRAWBERRY GANACHE

1. Wash then hull the strawberries. Process them with the caster sugar to make a coulis.
2. Heat the coulis in a saucepan, over a medium heat.
3. Break the chocolate up into pieces and place in a mixing bowl.
4. Once the coulis is hot, strain it through a fine sieve over the chocolate.
5. Gently combine to dissolve the chocolate and make the ganache smooth.
6. Decant into a suitable container and place in the refrigerator for at least 1 hour.

THE ASSEMBLY

Using a piping bag fitted with an 8 mm (³/₈ in) nozzle, fill half the macaron shells with strawberry ganache then assemble the macarons with the remaining shells. Place the macarons for an hour in the refrigerator.

RASPBERRY

A delicious mouthful of raspberry
A soft and slightly tart centre

MEMO

- For 40 macarons 3 cm (1¼ in) in diameter
- Preparation time ....50 minutes
- Drying time ....30 minutes
- Cooking time ....14 minutes
- Refrigeration time ...... 1 night + 1 hour
- Oven temperature ..150°C (300°F/Gas 2)

INGREDIENTS

- Ground almonds ....200 g (7 oz)
- Icing sugar......................200 g (7 oz)
- Water ....75 ml (2½ fl oz)
- Caster sugar ....200 g (7 oz)
- Egg whites ....2 × 80 g (2 × 2¾ oz)
- Raspberry pink colouring

Raspberry marmalade (make the day before)

- Caster sugar...175 g (6 oz)
  (or jam sugar .... 160 g (5¾ oz)
- Fresh or frozen raspberries...300 g (10½ oz)
- Lemon..½
- Pectin (jelly dessert powder)...15 g (½ oz)

STRUCTURE

Flamboyantly coloured shells that whet the appetite.
An intensely fruity centre.

Cook the raspberry marmalade until it reaches 104–105°C (219–221°F).

THE MACARONS

1. Process then carefully sift the *tant pour tant* (see pages 12–13). Set aside.

2. In a saucepan, bring the water and caster sugar to the boil. Without stirring, make sure the temperature of the resulting syrup doesn't go above 115°C (240°F).

3. Gently beat 80 g (2³/₄ oz) egg whites to soft peaks, then increase the beater speed once the temperature of the syrup passes 105°C (220°F). When the syrup reaches 115°C (240°F) remove the saucepan from the heat and pour the syrup in a thin stream into the beaten egg whites. Continue to beat the meringue for about 10 minutes, so that it cools a little.

4. Combine the *tant pour tant* with the remaining egg whites, making a smooth almond paste. Add one or two drops of pink colouring, for a more or less intense colour according to preference.

5. Using a flexible spatula, incorporate about a third of the meringue into the almond paste in order to loosen the mixture a little, then add the rest of the meringue, carefully working the batter.

6. Fill a piping bag fitted with an 8 mm (³/₈ in) nozzle with batter. Attach the baking paper to each baking tray by placing small dots of batter in the corners. Pipe out small, regular and well-spaced rounds, about the size of a walnut. Lightly tap the bottom of the trays and allow to dry at room temperature for 30 minutes.

7. Preheat the oven to 150°C (300°F/Gas 2).

8. Bake in the oven for 14 minutes. When they come out of the oven, carefully place the baking paper on a dampened benchtop: the shells will be easier to remove.

THE RASPBERRY MARMALADE

1. In a saucepan, dissolve the caster sugar with 100 ml (3 ¹/₂ fl oz) water, then bring the syrup to the boil.

2. Check the temperature using a sugar thermometer. Once the syrup reaches 110°C (230°F), add the raspberries (if using frozen raspberries, thaw them beforehand and add their juice), the juice of the half lemon and the pectin. Combine using a spatula so you lightly crush the raspberries.

3. Cook over a medium heat, monitoring the temperature. Once it reaches 104–105°C (219–221°F), remove the marmalade from the heat and decant it into a suitable container.

4. Allow to cool for 15 minutes at room temperature, then refrigerate for at least 1 hour.

Tip: to save time, use store-bought raspberry jam and stir in a few fresh raspberry pieces.

THE ASSEMBLY

Using a piping bag fitted with an 8 mm (³/₈ in) nozzle, fill half the macaron shells with the raspberry marmalade then assemble the macarons with the remaining shells. Store in an airtight container.

LEMON

A macaron that's yellow, smooth and shiny
A lemon filling that will remind you of the tang of lemon meringue pie

MEMO

- For 40 macarons 3 cm (1¹/₄ in) in diameter
- Preparation time............... 50 minutes
- Drying time...................... 30 minutes
- Cooking time.................... 14 minutes
- Refrigeration time ....1 night + 1 hour
- Oven temperature .. 150°C (300°F/Gas 2)

INGREDIENTS

- Ground almonds...............200 g (7 oz)
- Icing sugar ....200 g (7 oz)
- Egg whites............ 2 × 80 g (2 × 2³/₄ oz)
- Caster sugar.....................200 g (7 oz)
- Water........................ 75 ml (2¹/₂ fl oz)
- Yellow colouring

Lemon cream (make the day before)

- Lemon or lime juice .... 200 ml (7 fl oz)
- Eggs... 3
- Egg yolks 6
- Caster sugar... 75 g (2¹/₂ oz)
- Butter .... 110 g (3³/₄ oz)
- White chocolate .... 125 g (4¹/₂ oz)

STRUCTURE

Crisp and tart at the same time, this macaron relieves gourmands of their guilty feelings with a fresh creamy filling that seems lighter than a ganache or lemon curd.

Off the heat, incorporate the butter and white chocolate into the lemon cream.

THE MACARONS

1. Process then carefully sift the *tant pour tant* (see pages 12–13). Set aside.
2. In a saucepan, bring the water and caster sugar to the boil. Without stirring, make sure the temperature of the resulting syrup doesn't go above 115°C (240°F).
3. Gently beat 80 g (2³/₄ oz) egg whites to soft peaks, then increase the beater speed once the temperature of the syrup passes 105°C (220°F). When the syrup reaches 115°C (240°F) remove the saucepan from the heat and pour the syrup in a thin stream into the beaten egg whites. Continue to beat the meringue for about 10 minutes, so that it cools down a little.
4. Combine the *tant pour tant* with the remaining egg whites, making a smooth almond paste. Add one or two drops of yellow colouring for a more or less intense colour according to preference.
5. Using a flexible spatula, incorporate about a third of the meringue into the almond paste in order to loosen the mixture a little, then add the rest of the meringue, carefully working the batter.
6. Fill a piping bag fitted with an 8 mm (³/₈ in) nozzle with batter. Attach the baking paper to each baking tray by placing small dots of batter in the corners. Pipe out small, regular and well-spaced rounds, about the size of a walnut. Lightly tap the bottom of the trays and allow to form a crust at room temperature for 30 minutes.
7. Preheat the oven to 150°C (300°F/Gas 2).
8. Bake in the oven for 14 minutes. When they come out of the oven, carefully place the baking paper on a dampened benchtop: the shells will be easier to remove.

THE LEMON CREAM

1. Heat the lemon or lime juice in a saucepan, over a low heat.
2. Beat the eggs and egg yolks vigorously with the caster sugar in a mixing bowl. Pour the hot lemon juice over this mixture, then return the combined mixture to a low heat until it thickens, stirring continuously for about 3 to 4 minutes.
3. Remove from the heat and incorporate the butter and the white chocolate, chopped into small pieces. Mix well so the whole mixture is smooth.
4. Decant the cream into an airtight container then place in the refrigerator for at least 1 hour.

Tip: to save time, use store-bought lemon curd in place of the lemon cream.

THE ASSEMBLY

Using a piping bag with an 8 mm (³/₈ in) nozzle, fill half the macaron shells with lemon cream then assemble the macarons with the remaining shells. Place them in the refrigerator for an hour.

CHAPTER 3

SPECIALTY
MACARONS

*More ways to use the combination of almond, sugar and egg whites
to make macarons and other little authentic delicacies.*

UNCOOKED-SUGAR SHELLS

A basic technique that's certainly quicker
but also a more delicate operation

MEMO	INGREDIENTS	STRUCTURE
· For 40 macarons 3 cm (1¹/₄ in) in diameter	· Ground almonds............... .... 125 g (4¹/₂ oz)	· The shells are not as smooth and shiny as ones made from a sugar-syrup mixture.
· Preparation time............... .... 30 minutes	· Icing sugar ...220 g (7³/₄ oz) · Egg whites ....100 g (3¹/₂ oz)	· The colours tend to become paler when cooked.
· Drying time..... 40 minutes · Cooking time....12 minutes · Oven temperature............. .... 170°C (325°F/Gas 3)	· Caster sugar........25 g (1 oz)	· Be careful when working the batter!

THE MACARONS

1. Process together the ground almonds and icing sugar, then carefully sift the mixture (this is called the *tant pour tant*: see pages 12-13). Whisk the egg whites into soft peaks with an electric beater. Once they are nice and frothy, add the caster sugar and continue to beat for about 10 minutes to break up the structure of the egg whites and firm up the meringue.

2. Incorporate the *tant pour tant* into the meringue and, using a spatula, work the batter to loosen it and "break" the beaten egg whites. The batter should be smooth and slowly resume its shape when lifted up and allowed to fall back on itself.

3. Fill a piping bag fitted with an 8 mm (³/₈ in) nozzle with batter. Attach the baking paper to each baking tray by placing small dots of batter in the corners. Pipe out small, regular and well-spaced rounds, about the size of a walnut. Lightly tap the bottom of the trays and allow to dry at room temperature for 40 minutes.

4. Preheat the oven to 170°C (325°F/Gas 3).

5. Bake in the oven for 12 minutes, lowering the temperature of the oven to 150°C (300°F/Gas 2) for the last 5 minutes. When they come out of the oven, carefully place the baking paper on a dampened benchtop: the shells will be easier to remove.

MACARONS DE NANCY

*A delicious treat made from a delicate mixture of egg white, sugar
and ground almonds, dating from the 17th century*

MEMO

- For 45 macarons 3 cm
  (1¹/₄ in) in diameter
- Preparation time ....
  .... 15 minutes
- Drying time ..... 30 minutes
- Cooking time .... 15 minutes
- Oven temperature ....
  .... 180°C (350°F/Gas 4)

INGREDIENTS

- Ground almonds ....
  .... 250 g (9 oz)
- Icing sugar   320 g (11¹/₄ oz)
- Vanilla extract .... 3 drops
- Egg whites 4

STRUCTURE

- Pretty round shells,
  crackled and coloured.
- Enjoyed as is, like
  an almond biscuit or
  shortbread, but with no
  flour!

THE MACARONS

1. Process the ground almonds and icing sugar (this is called the *tant pour tant*: see pages
12–13). Add the vanilla extract, then incorporate the egg whites, lightly beaten to soft peaks, until
you have a dense, smooth batter.

2. Line a baking tray with some baking paper, attaching it with small dots of batter in the corners.
Fill a piping bag fitted with an 8 mm (³/₈ in) nozzle with batter, then make small regular rounds
about 2 cm (³/₄ in) in diameter and spaced about 5 cm (2 in) apart. Lightly tap the bottom of the
tray with your hand and allow to dry at room temperature for 30 minutes.

3. Preheat the oven to 180°C (350°F/Gas 4).

4. Place in the oven, lower the temperature straight away to 150°C (300°F/Gas 2), and cook the
macarons for 15 minutes. The shells should be a lovely golden brown.

5. Gently place the sheet of baking paper on a dampened benchtop to stop the cooking process,
then remove the macarons using a metal spatula.

NOTES

Macarons de Nancy keep well for a few days in an airtight container.

AMARETTI

Considered to be THE Italian macaron, this little biscuit, both dry and tender, is made using sweet or bitter almonds (hence its name)

MEMO	INGREDIENTS	STRUCTURE
· For about 35 macarons · Preparation time............... ....15 minutes · Cooking time....12 minutes · Oven temperature............. .... 180°C (350°F/Gas 4)	· Ground almonds............... ....200 g (7 oz) · Icing sugar ...150 g (5¹/₂ oz) (plus extra for dusting) · Egg whites......................1 · Bitter almond extract ....1 tsp · Amaretto liqueur .....1 tbsp	· Simpler and quicker to make than French macarons. · Amaretti keep much better and improve over time.

THE MACARONS

1. Process the ground almonds and icing sugar together, (this is called the *tant pour tant*: see pages 12–13) then incorporate the egg white, almond extract and amaretto. Combine vigorously until you have a smooth batter.

2. Preheat the oven to 180°C (350°F/Gas 4).

3. Shape small walnut-sized balls of the mixture and arrange them on a baking tray lined with baking paper, spacing them about 5 cm (2 in) apart.

4. Lightly pinch the top of each ball to make small points and place in the oven straight away. Cook for 12 minutes and dust with icing sugar as soon as they come out of the oven.

HAZELNUT

A natural autumnal colour
The macaron shells and filling are made using ground hazelnuts

MEMO

- For 40 macarons 3 cm (1¼ in) in diameter
- Preparation time............... .... 50 minutes
- Drying time..... 30 minutes
- Cooking time....14 minutes
- Refrigeration time ...1 hour
- Oven temperature .... 150°C (300°F/Gas 2)

INGREDIENTS

- Ground almonds............... .... 100 g (3½ oz)
- Ground hazelnuts.............. .... 100 g (3½ oz)
- Icing sugar ...... 200 g (7 oz)
- Water .... 75 ml (2½ fl oz)
- Caster sugar..... 200 g (7 oz)
- Egg whites......................... ....2 × 80 g (2 × 2¾ oz)

Hazelnut cream
- Ground almonds............... .... 60 g (2¼ oz)
- Shelled or ground hazelnuts .... 100 g (3½ oz)
- Softened butter 250 g (9 oz)
- Icing sugar ...... 140 g (5 oz)

THE MACARONS

1. Finely process the ground almonds, ground hazelnuts and icing sugar then sift (this is called the *tant pour tant*: see pages 12–13). The residue left in the sieve can be used to sprinkle over the macarons.

2. In a saucepan, bring the water and caster sugar to the boil. Without stirring, make sure the temperature of the resulting syrup doesn't go above 115°C (240°F).

3. Make an Italian meringue using 80 g (2¾ oz) egg whites (see method page 57).

4. Mix the *tant pour tant* and the remaining egg whites to make a smooth paste.
Using a flexible spatula, incorporate about a third of the meringue into this paste, to loosen it a little, then add the rest of the meringue, carefully working the batter.

5. Fill a piping bag fitted with an 8 mm (³⁄₈ in) nozzle with batter. Attach some baking paper to each baking tray by placing small dots of batter in the corners. Pipe out small, regular and well-spaced rounds, about the size of a walnut. Sprinkle the macarons, if desired, with the *tant pour tant* residue, then tap the bottom of the trays and allow them to form a crust for 30 minutes.

6. Preheat the oven to 150°C (300°F/Gas 2). Bake in the oven for 14 minutes, then gently place the baking paper on a dampened benchtop: the shells will be easier to remove.

THE HAZELNUT CREAM

1. Process the hazelnuts with the ground almonds.

2. Beat the softened butter vigorously, using a whisk or an electric beater, to give it a very smooth and creamy texture. Add the icing sugar and beat again. Incorporate the hazelnut–almond mixture and whisk again for a few minutes to aerate the cream and give it lightness.

3. Using a piping bag fitted with an 8 mm (³⁄₈ in) nozzle, fill half the shells with the cream, then assemble the macarons with the remaining shells. Refrigerate the macarons for an hour.

DOUBLE PISTACHIO

A shell sprinkled with ground pistachio
A more or less intensely flavoured filling according to taste

MEMO	INGREDIENTS	STRUCTURE
· For 40 macarons 3 cm (1¼ in) in diameter · Preparation time .... 50 minutes · Drying time ..... 30 minutes · Cooking time .... 14 minutes · Oven temperature .... 150°C (300°F/Gas 2)	· Unsalted shelled pistachios .... 120 g (4¼ oz) · Ground almonds............... .... 80 g (2¾ oz) · Icing sugar ...... 200 g (7 oz) · Water .... 75 ml (2½ fl oz) · Caster sugar..... 200 g (7 oz) · Egg whites......................... .... 2 × 80 g (2 × 2¾ oz)	· A crisp shell with a natural taste and colour. · A creamy centre with small nuggets of pistachio.

THE MACARONS

1. Finely process the pistachios with the ground almonds and icing sugar (this is called the *tant pour tant*: see pages 12–13). Set aside. The residue left in the sieve can be used to sprinkle over the macarons.

2. In a saucepan, bring the water and caster sugar to the boil. Without stirring, check that the temperature of the resulting syrup doesn't go above 115°C (240°F).

3. Gently beat 80 g (2¾ oz) egg whites to soft peaks, then increase the beater speed once the temperature of the syrup passes 105°C (220°F). When the syrup reaches 115°C (240°F) remove the saucepan from the heat and pour the syrup in a thin stream into the beaten egg whites. Continue to beat the meringue for about 10 minutes, so that it cools a little.

4. Combine the *tant pour tant* and the remaining egg whites to make a smooth paste.

5. Using a flexible spatula, incorporate about a third of the meringue into this paste, in order to loosen it a little, then add the rest of the meringue, carefully working the batter.

6. Fill a piping bag fitted with an 8 mm (³⁄₈ in) nozzle with batter. Attach a sheet of baking paper to each baking tray by placing small dots of batter in the corners. Pipe out small, regular and well-spaced rounds, about the size of a walnut. Sprinkle them lightly, if desired, with the *tant pour tant* residue, then lightly tap the bottom of the trays and allow to form a crust at room temperature for 30 minutes.

7. Preheat the oven to 150°C (300°F/Gas 2). Bake in the oven for 14 minutes then gently place the baking paper on a dampened benchtop: the shells will be easier to remove.

8. Using a piping bag fitted with an 8mm (³⁄₈ in) nozzle, generously fill half of the shells with the filling of your choice (see page 65) then assemble the macarons with the remaining shells.

WALNUT

A crisp and melting texture
A natural colour
Both the shells and filling are made using ground walnuts

MEMO

- For 40 macarons 3 cm (1 ¼ in) in diameter
- Preparation time .... 50 minutes
- Drying time ..... 30 minutes
- Cooking time .... 14 minutes
- Oven temperature ....150°C (300°F/Gas 2)

INGREDIENTS

- Walnuts .... 100 g (3 ½ oz)
- Ground almonds .... 100 g (3 ½ oz)
- Icing sugar ...... 200 g (7 oz)
- Water .... 75 ml (2 ½ fl oz)
- Caster sugar ..... 200 g (7 oz)
- Egg whites .... 2 × 80 g (2 × 2 ¾ oz)

Walnut cream
- Walnuts .... 100 g (3 ½ oz)
- Ground almonds .... 60 g (2 ¼ oz)
- Softened butter .... 250 g (9 oz)
- Icing sugar ..... 140 g (5 oz)

THE MACARONS

1. Finely process the walnuts with the ground almonds and icing sugar (this is called the *tant pour tant*: see pages 12–13). The residue left in the sieve can be used to sprinkle over the macarons.
2. In a saucepan, bring the water and caster sugar to the boil. Without stirring, check that the temperature of the resulting syrup doesn't go above 115°C (240°F).
3. Make an Italian meringue using 80 g (2¾ oz) egg whites (see method page 57).
4. Combine the *tant pour tant* with the remaining egg whites to make a smooth paste. Using a flexible spatula, incorporate about a third of the meringue into this paste, in order to loosen it a little, then add the rest of the meringue, working the batter.
5. Fill a piping bag fitted with an 8 mm (³/₈ in) nozzle with batter. Attach the baking paper to the baking trays by placing dots of batter in each corner.
6. Pipe out small, regular and well-spaced rounds, about the size of a walnut. Lightly sprinkle the macaron shells, if desired, with the *tant pour tant* residue, then lightly tap the bottom of the trays and allow to form a crust at room temperature for 30 minutes.
7. Preheat the oven to 150°C (300°F/Gas 2). Bake in the oven for 14 minutes. When they come out of the oven, carefully place the baking paper on a dampened benchtop.

THE WALNUT CREAM

1. Process the walnuts with the ground almonds.
2. Beat the softened butter vigorously until smooth and creamy. Add the icing sugar and beat again. Incorporate the ground nuts and whisk for a few minutes to aerate the cream and give it lightness.
3. Using a piping bag fitted with an 8 mm (³/₈ in) nozzle, fill half the shells with cream, then assemble the macarons with the remaining shells.

HONEY

*Pearly with powder or gold leaf, filled with a smooth honey
and bee-pollen cream, could these macarons have beneficial powers?*

MEMO

- For 40 macarons 3 cm (1¹/₄ in) in diameter
- Preparation time.............................. 40 minutes
- Drying time ..... 30 minutes
- Cooking time ....14 minutes
- Oven temperature .... 150°C (300°F/Gas 2)

INGREDIENTS

- Ground almonds............... .... 200 g (7 oz)
- Icing sugar ...... 200 g (7 oz)
- Water .... 75 ml (2 ¹/₂ fl oz)
- Caster sugar..... 140 g (5 oz)
- Honey .... 60 g (2 ¹/₄ oz)
- Egg whites......................... .... 2 × 80 g (2 × 2 ³/₄ oz)
- Caramel colouring

- Edible shimmer powder or gold leaf (optional)

- *Honey cream*
- Egg yolks........................ 2
- Honey .... 60 g (2 ¹/₄ oz)
- Mascarpone..... 250 g (9 oz)
- Bee-pollen granules (see glossary) .... 50 g (1 ³/₄ oz)

THE MACARONS

1. Process then finely sift the *tant pour tant*, (see pages 12–13) and set aside.

2. In a saucepan, bring the water, caster sugar and honey to the boil. Without stirring, make sure the temperature of the syrup doesn't go above 115°C (240°F).

3. Make an Italian meringue with 80 g (2 ³/₄ oz) egg whites (see method page 57).

4. Combine the *tant pour tant* with the remaining egg whites, making a smooth almond paste. Add a little caramel colouring. Using a flexible spatula, incorporate about a third of the meringue into the almond paste to loosen it a little, then add the rest of the meringue, carefully working the batter.

5. Fill a piping bag fitted with an 8 mm (³/₈ in) nozzle with batter. Attach a sheet of baking paper to each baking tray by placing small dots of batter in the corners. Pipe out regular and well-spaced rounds about the size of a walnut. Lightly tap the bottom of the trays and allow the macarons to form a crust at room temperature for 30 minutes.

6. Preheat the oven to 150°C (300°F/Gas 2). Bake for 14 minutes, then place the baking paper on a dampened benchtop: the shells will be easier to remove. Using your finger, give half the shells a pearly sheen using the shimmer powder or decorate them with gold leaf (optional).

THE HONEY CREAM

1. In a mixing bowl, lightly whisk the egg yolks and honey, then add the mascarpone and beat again. Add the bee-pollen granules and combine more gently.

2. Using a piping bag fitted with an 8 mm (³/₈ in) nozzle, fill half the macaron shells with honey cream then assemble the macarons with the remaining shells.

APPENDIX

GLOSSARY

AGAR-AGAR A mucilaginous substance also known as "China grass" or "kanten". A seaweed extract, agar-agar is available as thin translucent strips in various colours, as blocks or in powdered form.

ANTIOXIDANTS Nutrients that capture free radicals in the body.

BAIN-MARIE A cooking method used to melt chocolate gently. It is achieved by placing a container with the pieces of chocolate in it above a saucepan of simmering water.

BATTER A blend of various ingredients used to make a dish, especially in baking.

BEAT Mix ingredients together vigorously using a whisk, fork or electric beater.

BEAT THE WHITES TO SOFT PEAKS Beat the egg whites with a whisk or electric beater until they have a firm consistency and can form a peak on the whisk.

BEE-POLLEN GRANULES Provide a subtle honey flavour. Available at good health food shops and online stores.

BICARBONATE OF SODA A raising agent.

BUTTER CREAM An emulsified preparation made from butter, sugar and eggs, flavoured according to preference.

CALCIUM An element found in several foods (milk, butter, eggs, chocolate).

CARBOHYDRATES These represent a source of energy for our body. There are 3 categories of carbohydrate: simple carbohydrates, complex carbohydrates and dietary fibre.

CAROTENE An orange-coloured pigment.

CHALAZAE Twisted threads of albumin protein located on each side of the egg yolk, maintaining its position in the centre of the white.

CHANTILLY CREAM, WHIPPED CREAM To make chantilly or whipped cream, the cream needs to be well chilled. The whisk and bowl should be placed in the freezer beforehand.

CHOLESTEROL An essential component of our cells. Animal-derived foods are high in cholesterol. High blood cholesterol levels are the result of an unhealthy lifestyle and can lead to cardiovascular disease.

CREAM Vigorously whisk eggs with sugar until the mixture becomes pale.

CROÛTAGE (DRYING TIME) This is an essential stage for obtaining smooth macaron shells. It takes about 30 minutes at room temperature and allows the shells to develop a thin film on top. This film helps the macarons to cook more evenly.

EMULSION A mixture of two liquids (for example, eggs and melted butter).

FATS These provide energy to our body. They are divided into 3 categories: saturated fats, monounsaturated fats and polyunsaturated fats.

FIBRE Carbohydrates that are essential to the healthy functioning of the digestive system. Foods high in fibre are low in fat and kilojoules. They give a feeling of fullness, slowing down the appetite.

FLAVONOIDS Plant-derived substances that form part of the antioxidant group. Found in chocolate.

FOOD COLOURING An additive used to change the colour of a commercial food product or cooked dish, throughout or just on the surface. It is available in different forms: liquid, powder or paste.

FRUCTOSE A simple sugar found in fruits, honey and some vegetables. It is absorbed more slowly than glucose.

GANACHE A pastry cream used to decorate desserts, fill cakes or sweets, and make petits-fours.

GLUCOSE A simple sugar.

IRON An energising trace element essential to the body's system.

KILOJOULES (kJ) Reserves of energy. Kilojoules not used by the body are stored in the form of fat.

LECITHIN An emulsifier used to bind various ingredients. It softens and increases the volume of food preparations by acting on the elasticity and flexibility of gluten. It also promotes the binding process between water and fats.

MACARONAGE (WORKING THE BATTER) This is the incorporation of the meringue into the almond paste. It is a delicate operation because the success of the macaron shells depends on obtaining the right batter texture.

MAGNESIUM An essential trace element for preventing tiredness and stress. Chocolate is high in magnesium. It is also found in hazelnuts, almonds, grains and spinach, among other foods.

MARMALADE A preparation of fruit, left whole or cut into pieces, macerated for 24 hours in sugar and cooked to the consistency of a jelly.

MINERALS These are responsible for the smooth functioning of our bodies' systems in association with other nutrients.

NOZZLE Made from stainless steel, tin plate or plastic, these are cone-shaped and fit into the end of a piping bag. The nozzle's opening, in different sizes (round or flat, smooth, serrated or fluted), allow the mixture in the bag to be shaped.

ORGEAT SYRUP A flavoured syrup made from almonds, sugar and sometimes flavoured with rosewater or orange-flower water. Available from specialty beverage suppliers.

OVALBUMIN The element in egg whites that aerates, thickens and solidifies.

PECTIN A natural gelling substance, made of carbohydrate, which is present in various plants — in particular in the juice of certain fruits. It helps to "set" jams or jellies.

PHOSPHATE A food additive, used as a stabiliser.

PIPING BAG (WITH NOZZLE) An instrument used in cooking to distribute substances with a paste-like consistency. Contents are placed inside the cone-shaped bag, then compressed and expelled via the tip in mounded shapes or lengths.

POTASSIUM Essential element contained in fruits and vegetables. Helps reduce blood pressure.

PROTEIN Found in many foods. May be plant- or animal-based.

SACCHAROSE Sugar extracted from sugar beets or sugar cane.

SEPARATING EGGS Separating the egg white from the egg yolk.

SHELL A small meringue preparation, incorporating ground almonds or hazelnuts (as in the classic *pâte à progrès, à succès*), used for making petits-fours or gâteaus; petit-four shells are joined together using a fruit marmalade, flavoured butter cream or chestnut purée (*crème de marrons*), then eventually glazed with fondant icing.

SIFT To pass dry ingredients through a sieve. When making cakes, flour and cocoa need to be sifted to avoid lumps. Any raising agent should be sifted with the flour. That way it will be distributed more evenly and the batter will rise evenly.

SILICONE SPATULA A spatula that is resistant to high temperatures and an effective bowl scraper.

SODIUM OR SODIUM CHLORIDE Salt. Too much salt in the diet is a risk factor for blood pressure.

TANT POUR TANT A mixture of equal proportions of icing sugar and ground almonds, used by professional pastry cooks or confectioners for making cake batters, petit-four shells, etc.

TARTARIC ACID One of the ingredients in baking powder.

TITANIUM DIOXIDE Also called titanium white, this is a white pigment. Non-toxic, it is produced from a chloride process.

TRACE ELEMENTS Zinc, selenium, magnesium, copper, iron ... essential to our bodies' systems.

VITAMINS Found in fruits and vegetables. A varied and balanced diet is necessary for an adequate vitamin intake.

TABLE OF CONTENTS

ACKNOWLEDGEMENTS

A big thank you
To Fred, for his pretty photos and good taste!
To Christophe, faithful friend and partner, always there to share these moments.
To Carine, always ready to "macaron", day or night!
To Sandra, for her kindness and for letting me rummage through her cupboards ...
To all my team, customers and friends at Café Noir for their support.
To the whole Marabout team for their trust.
www.cafenoirparis.com

BIBLIOGRAPHY

Since my first attempts at Pavillon Ledoyen, where I learned this delicate art among many other things, it is now over a decade that I have been "macaroning".
The recipes in the book are the fruit of several perfecting processes, whether of the cooking time, the temperature of the oven or the little tricks that emerge from many more or less successful batches of macarons, but also of various investigations which allowed me to get a better understanding of the ingredients of this delicacy.
I've thus brought together in this manual the results of these many experiences and experiments so that you can understand, step by step, all the tips and methods I have learned over the years.